Great Passages of the

BIBLE

Salvation from Beginning to End

Everett Leadingham, Editor

Though this book is designed for group study, it is also intended for personal enjoyment and spiritual growth. A leader's guide is available from your local bookstore or your publisher.

Beacon Hill Press of Kansas City
Kansas City, Missouri

Editor
Everett Leadingham

Assistant Editor
Charlie L. Yourdon

Executive Editor
Randy Cloud

Editorial Committee
Philip Baisley
Carolyn Clements
Randy Cloud
David Higle
Everett Leadingham
Thomas Mayse
Larry Morris
Charlie L. Yourdon

Cover design by
Kevin Williamson

Copyright 1997
Beacon Hill Press of Kansas City
Kansas City, Missouri
ISBN: 083-411-6871
Printed in the United States of America

Contents

Preface

This book has been a long time in the making. Everyone involved agreed that a study of some great passages of Scripture was indeed a good idea. However, the process of agreeing on only 13 was a difficult one. Of all the majestic and inspiring contents of the Bible, how could we choose the 13 "greatest" ones?

After many discussions and much prayer, we found a way. The most important theme in the Bible is the history of salvation revealed in its pages. All along the way, from beginning to end, the Scriptures reveal how God provided a way of salvation for the human beings He created and loved so much. Certain passages of the Bible tell this story of salvation more directly than others do. We have chosen 13 of those clear scriptures to discuss in this book. As you read each of the chapters in this book, you will want to have your own Bible open as well, allowing the words of these timeless passages to impact your heart anew.

As we move from Genesis 1, through the Old Testament, into the New Testament, and finally into Revelation, we will track the story of salvation as God more fully reveals His plan passage by passage. This is a story about God and about us but, more importantly, about God's loving concern for our salvation from sin and His call to live holy lives.

Genesis 1—3

INTRODUCTION

Naming a book after the first word or two of the text was common in ancient times. When 70 scholars translated the Hebrew Scriptures into Greek, the word for "beginning" became the first word of the first book. That name has survived into our English Bibles as "Genesis."

When we understand the narratives in Genesis, we have a basis for grasping the message of the entire Bible. Genesis is the story of salvation as God revealed himself to the generations following Abraham. The rest of the Bible shows how He continued to disclose His love and mercy to Abraham's descendants, even down to Jesus of Nazareth, whom we know as our Savior.

Among all the scientific data and theological confusion of our time, we can easily forget what Scripture has taught unapologetically for thousands of years. Scripture makes no argument trying to prove that God exists. The Bible simply starts telling of His mighty acts with the words, "In the beginning God . . ." God is the Creator of the beautiful world we enjoy inhabiting. God is also the Source of our salvation from the not-so-beautiful side of our world and of ourselves.

Going back to the starting point is an appropriate way to begin any study of history. Nothing—not even we humans—would exist without God. So it is proper that our study of the story of salvation begins—and ends—in the One who was there at the beginning. The first three chapters of Genesis show us how we got here and remind us why we need a Savior.

CHAPTER 1

The Beginning of Our Story

by Jon Johnston

SOME YEARS AGO a TV host had this interchange with a little girl:

"Miss, what is your favorite Bible story?"

"The story of Edem and Av."

"You mean Adam and Eve."

"No, Edem and Av."

"What happened to them?"

"Well, they got in *big* trouble for eating cherries off a bush."

"What did they do then?"

"They hid under a park bench—but God found them all right."

"What did God do to them after He found them?"

"He made them into Protestants!"

Like our little friend, we all have some familiarity with events described in the first few chapters of Genesis. Still, also like her, we may have our facts a bit whopper jawed.

Genesis 1—3 unwraps the narrative of our first parents. It comes to us in the form of a captivating, three-part drama: creation, enticement to sin, and punishment.

Let's focus on each of these closely: first, to clearly understand what occurred; second, to grasp some valuable lessons that can bring proper responses to this crucial story.

Creation: A Generous Treasure

Try to imagine a time when nothing existed. No stars. No earth. No oceans or trees. It's hard to fathom such a time.

All cultures possess folklore and fables that attempt to shed light on how life started. Modern skeptics contend that our natural order evolved by chance. What does Scripture proclaim? In a word, the spotlight shines on our supreme, majestic, all-knowing, all-powerful God—who, together with His Son, created all things (John 1:1-3).

Forget about finding arguments that prove His existence. Our Bible emphatically and consistently affirms in poetic and prophetic ways God's existence. Everything our Heavenly Father created was new, perfect, and not derived from anything that existed previously.

The creation story in Genesis emphasizes the orderliness of God's labor. He replaced the "formlessness" and "emptiness" of a world shrouded in "darkness" (1:2) with design, beauty, and purpose. And He did so in a very systematic manner.

First, God established this definite pattern for each of creation's six days: to start, a *creation command* ("Let there be light"); next, an *announcement of its effect* ("And it was so"); then *God's evaluation* ("And God saw that it was good"); followed by *God's naming* ("God called the light 'day'") and the *numbering of days* ("And there was evening, and there was morning—the fifth day").

Second, He channeled His creative energy into two crucial activities—activities that, in a real sense, parallel what He does for us when He comes into our hearts—*forming* and *filling*.

Forming. On days one through three, He created the heavens and the earth (v. 1), light (v. 3), the sky (vv. 7-8), land and seas (vv. 9-10), and vegetation (v. 11). He separated light from darkness (v. 4), water from water (v. 6), and water from sky (vv. 7-8). He gathered water from land (v. 9) and water from water—to form seas (v. 10).

Filling. On days four through six, He provided light (sun, moon, and stars) to dispel darkness in the sky and on earth (vv. 14-19). He created living creatures (birds and fish) to fill skies and seas (vv. 20-23) as well as others (livestock, wild animals, ground crawlers) to inhabit the land (vv. 24-25). He created humans to rule over all other creatures (vv. 26-27).

In contrast with all other things, His creation of humans was very special and distinctive. Here are a few reasons why:

First, our original parents were *created in God's image.* This probably does not refer to physical resemblance. God existed before anything physical came into being and is not bound by physical limitations. Rather, it pertains to the spiritual nature we all share: our intelligence, moral consciousness, and freedom of choice.

Second, Adam and Eve were given *a degree of dominion* over God's creation—vegetation and the "lesser creatures," such as fish, fowl, cattle, wild animals, and creeping crawlers (vv. 26, 29-30). God invited Adam to name members of the animal kingdom, an offer that further implied human supremacy (2:19-20).

Third, the Scriptures give *a more detailed account* of the creation of our original ancestors than all other life. Unlike all else, they had *separate creations.* Adam was formed from the earth's elements. Eve originated from Adam's own body, suggesting a unity between them. Both received a powerful *breath of God's Spirit.* Finally, God provided them residence on some *very special real estate*—a garden containing lush vegetation of indescribable beauty.

Now for some bad news: Things started to turn ugly

when Satan entered the picture. Let's track the downward spiral.

The Great Enticement to Sin

The honeymoon stage of any new relationship is almost always fun, exciting, promising. It's so for new students who enter the university where I teach. During orientation week, counselors provide personal guidance, administrators offer the warmest welcome, professors give encouragement. Some students conclude that higher education is a picnic—that is, until midterm examinations result in a jolting reality check.

Adam and Eve basked in ecstasy until the testing period began. Enter Satan, the devil—later identified as God's adversary and the evil tempter. He assumed the form of a serpent, described as "more crafty than any of the wild animals" (3:1).

Note how he gradually, but ever-so-skillfully, set his trap. Satan began by twisting God's words. "Did God really say, 'You must not eat from any tree?'" (v. 1). To Eve's credit, she confirmed that God had, indeed, commanded just that. She went on to add something Satan had conveniently but purposefully omitted: "and you must not touch it, or you will die" (v. 3). Then comes Satan's blatant challenge of God's words: "You will not surely die" (v. 4).

Not through yet, Satan pretends to know the motive behind God dispensing "incorrect" information. In a word, it was sheer, green-eyed jealousy. "For God knows that when you eat of it your eyes will be opened, and you will be like God, knowing good and evil" (v. 5).

Using her mental calculator, Eve began adding up the reasons why she should eat the fruit. Grand total: three. In her judgment, the fruit was: (1) good for food, (2) pleasant to her eye, and (3) desirable for attaining wisdom, for distinguishing good from evil as God could (v. 6).

It is important to note that Eve came up with the first

two, then added in Satan's single enticement. No surprise here. Whenever we decide to sin, we're likely to think up a ton of rationalizations. Feeling guilty, we grope for supporting arguments.

Is it time to draw the curtain on the story? Not quite. Misery likes miserable company. Unwilling to cave in alone, Eve handed the forbidden fruit to Adam. We have no record of Adam carefully weighing his alternatives. It seems to be a case of "see fruit—eat fruit."

Sin drags us down. This principle is easily seen in the steps to compromise surrounding the "first family's" fall. The first step was *casualness.* Eve began conversing with, and giving her undivided attention to, Satan. Next came *carelessness.* Eve corrected Satan initially but then passively accepted his lie concerning the "glorious effects" of consuming the fruit. The third step was *compulsiveness.* After hearing out the evil one, Eve tried to convince herself that eating was the thing to do. Then followed the final step, *callousness.* She became insensitive. Knowing that she had done wrong, she pulled Adam into her "ditch."

Is there anything about these steps that seems in the least bit familiar? I'm afraid so, unfortunately. Sin always extracts its toll. Let's see how it did for Adam and Eve.

The Gripping Toll of Punishment

Satan had clothed himself as a serpent—in order to deceive. Now, Adam and Eve clothed themselves in fig leaves—hiding the nakedness they had suddenly become ashamed of (3:7).

Clothing wasn't enough. After hearing God's voice in the distance, they rushed to hide "among the trees" (v. 8). How sad! Eden, once the site of joy and divine-human fellowship, had become the place of fear and human avoidance of the divine.

The inevitable confrontation took place. God called out, "Where are you?" (v. 9). Adam, realizing that he and

Eve were in trouble, began confessing his embarrassment about being in his birthday suit. God asked two questions: "Who told you that you were naked? Have you eaten from the tree that I commanded you *not* to eat from?" (v. 11, emphasis added).

It was stutter and shuffle time for Adam. Glancing down at Eve's guilty countenance, he blurted out, "The woman you put here with me—*she gave me* some fruit from the tree, and I ate it" (v. 12, emphasis added).

Turning to Eve, God asked, "What is this you have done?" (v. 13). Eve, who had been less than talkative since her fruit-sampling episode, managed an answer: "The serpent deceived me, and I ate" (v. 13). She figured if blaming worked for Adam, why shouldn't she give it a shot?

God was less than impressed or amused. How do we know? Everyone in the vicinity was served a generous cup of "hickory tea"—an old-fashioned word for stiff punishment.

For starters, in contrast to Adam and Eve, the serpent was given a curse. We're talking serious demotion—from craftiest of all wild animals to dust-eating crawler.

Then God "put enmity" (i.e., repulsion) between the woman and the serpent (v. 15). He broke up the cozy, chitchat relationship they had. Antagonism between people and serpents still symbolizes the outcome of the titanic struggle between God and Satan—played out in hearts throughout history.

OK, Eve, we're taking turns, and it's yours! Stand up, face God, and listen carefully. First, expect lots of pain during childbirth, more than the usual amount—if that wasn't enough already! "I will increase your pains" (v. 16) shows that the judgment of Eve fell on what was most uniquely hers as a woman.

Punishment No. 2: Expect to take a secondary role to your husband—in contrast to the primary one you assumed with the serpent and with your husband when you shoved the forbidden fruit in his hand. (Scores have misinterpreted this to sanction male superiority.)

Waiting for the other two to receive their punishment seemed, in itself, punishment enough for Adam. But now it's his turn.

First, the ground—his primary resource for livelihood—received a curse. It would relinquish its fruit reluctantly, requiring sweat and toil. Oh, yes, and in that same ground, "thorns and thistles" (v. 18) would grow like crazy.

Finally, God told Adam the clincher: You will die. Was he devastated? No doubt. But *we* need not be. Through redemption in Christ, once again, we have full and free access to the tree of eternal life (Revelation 2:7; 22:2, 14, 19)!

Genesis 1 through 3 is a two-part drama: great beginning—terrible ending. Yet within *each* scene we can learn valuable lessons. Let's lean in and examine some of the most crucial ones.

Our Response Is Grateful Worship

What of practical value does God's generous creation have to say to us? How can we cue into this ancient story in a way that will help us live lives that are more pleasing to our Maker?

The initial creation, admittedly spectacular, repeats in the cycles of nature. Nature "does her thing" every springtime, in fact, every moment of every single day. In essence, it's God trying to get our attention with a single message: "I love you."

Our Heavenly Father deserves our deepest gratitude, and that's what authentic worship is all about—acknowledging His incredible worth in humble thanksgiving.

Our Response Is Vigilance

Praise be to God for His gracious provision of salvation! Our "scarlet" hearts can, indeed, become "as white as snow" (Isaiah 1:18). We can experience joy unspeakable and full of glory!

However, make no mistake. Afterward, the serpent of evil never ceases trying to entice us. He continuously invites us to take big bites of "forbidden fruit," to succumb to sinful compromise. Furthermore, his approach involves a ton of sheer deceit. Hear Paul's words: "Satan himself masquerades as an angel of light" (2 Corinthians 11:14).

That's why we must take extra-special precautions. Our hearts must be on guard. Vigilance is a must. Peter declares: "Be self-controlled and *alert*. Your enemy the devil prowls around like a roaring lion looking for someone to devour" (1 Peter 5:8, emphasis added).

It is so easy to drift into nonvigilance, to be careless and manifest a cavalier attitude. In regard to Satan, we must be alert, armed, prepared to act, and reliant upon the Lord—our Shield and Defender. This means never underestimating our enemy's prowess. Or his persistence. Or his abilities of deception.

Like Humpty Dumpty, Adam and Eve took a great fall. Be well-assured, the same fate awaits us unless we stay on our spiritual toes!

Our Response Is Grieving but with Hope

Only someone with a vile heart or sick mind delights in seeing people suffer for their sins. Such times are tragic on all counts, especially when red warning flags have gone unheeded and when enemies of righteousness celebrate.

How should we most appropriately respond to those who have fallen? Make excuses? ("After all, we're all only human.") Harshly criticize? ("They deserve God's wrath!")

Neither of these is good or right. The first overlooks the biblical standard of accountability; the second discounts Christ's stern warnings against judging.

Far superior to these, as loving, compassionate believers, we must grieve. Someone once said: "Our hearts must be broken by the things that break the heart of God." And sin is No. 1 on the list.

He sorrows for those who refuse His gift of grace, those who opt for Satan's chains rather than His crown of glory. So must we—continuously and fervently.

Yet along with our grieving, we must maintain a resilient, buoyant hope—a hope that sees far beyond the present, because it is generated from a heart that the Savior has enlightened. Paul underscores this crucial truth when he tells the Ephesians, "I pray also that the eyes of your heart may be enlightened in order that you may know the hope to which he has called you" (Ephesians 1:18).

It all comes down to our perspective—whether it's one of gloom and doom or hope and anticipation—regardless of what we have done or how God has reprimanded us for disobeying Him. No ditch need permanently entrap us.* We need only invite Him to touch "the eyes of our heart" so that we see our circumstances as He does, allowing Him to change what needs to be changed.

Put another way, God will help us to reframe our life's picture. We can't undo the past, alter others' wills, or receive miracles on demand. But God's new frame around that picture can make everything new. We can cope. We have hope. So, we can get unstuck and, with His tender and wise assistance, live the rest of our lives as "new creations!"

We must not take punishment for sin lightly, with a flippant, cavalier attitude. Instead, we must grieve as our Lord did when He foresaw the devastating consequences of Jerusalem's sins (Matthew 23:37).

However, it is crucial that we not stop there—stuck in sorrow. God didn't, even after seeing His Son die for our sins. The Cross became, as one put it, "God's eternal plus sign." Sorrow turned to joy; despair changed to hope. He reframed the world's most tragic event, and it became the reason for our greatest optimism.

The same principle holds for Adam and Eve's punishment. Admittedly, it was tragic. Their sentence was harsh, even though handed down by our loving God. Nevertheless, hope was not buried. This same Heavenly Father refused to abandon them. Rather, He continued to offer loving-kindness and tender mercy. He only wished for their best and encouraged them to turn from sin and get on with serving Him.

Plan B? Yes. But potentially a great plan B!

It's God's Style

My heart is warmed when I consider the "lives of broken pieces" that Christ *re*assembles, *re*directs, and *re*energizes. Paul gleefully persecuted Christians, then became the missionary of missionaries to the Gentiles. John Newton piloted slave ships, then ended up writing "Amazing Grace." Chuck Colson became enmeshed in the Watergate scandal, then began a prison ministry that touches the lives of thousands.

Our God never gives up on us, as long as we have breath and a pulse. His mercy and grace are lovingly offered, no matter how deeply we have sunk—or how tightly we are stuck. There is always hope of reconciliation. Always! God relentlessly, though never intrusively, pursues us until the end. Offering us unconditional love and acceptance. Offering us our *only* true hope!

If we respond in repentance and faith, He'll chart us on life's very best course. Sure, at times we may unfortunately settle for plan B—as Adam and Eve did. But this isn't the end of the world. Scores are marvelously saved later in life and experience incredible fulfillment in their remaining days.

As Reuben Welch says: "It's *never* 'get in or get out'; instead, it's *always* 'get in—get in!'" On this side of death, it's never too late!

And if we have decided to "get in," when we die,

we'll be warmly welcomed into that glorious Kingdom that He has so carefully and lavishly prepared for us. A place that's infinitely more beautiful and magnificent than even Adam and Eve's original neighborhood.

No truth is more certain. No certainty is more comforting.

About the author: Jon Johnston, Ph.D., is professor of sociology, anthropology, and social psychology at Pepperdine University, Malibu, California. He serves as president of the Association of Nazarene Sociologists of Religion.

---

*Jon Johnston, *Stuck in a Sticky World: Learning to See God's Best in Life's Worst* (Joplin, Mo.: College Press, 1996).

Genesis 15

INTRODUCTION

Throughout Scripture we find recurring themes that wrap themselves in and around the stories about God's people: faithfulness, loving-kindness, obedience, love, grace, fellowship, worship. Once we have grasped these key concepts, we have come a long way in understanding the heart of the Bible. And all of these important ideas are contained in one word: *covenant.*

Many feel the Bible is a mind-boggling array of unrelated promises, prohibitions, and personalities. They can fail to see that there is a consistent thread running throughout the story of God's dealings with His people. This thread is the covenant that God initiates between himself and Abraham in Genesis 15.

Another word for covenant is *testament,* and in fact the rest of the Old and New *Testaments* builds on what takes place in Genesis 15. The covenant we will read about in this passage is the same covenant that was renewed with Moses and the Israelites at Sinai. And it is a part of the same covenant He made centuries later by offering His only Son as a final sign and seal that God wants, more than anything else, to live in close relationship with His people.

Genesis 15 is one of the great passages of the Bible because it so clearly shows the loving, promise-making and promise-keeping character of God. The covenant made here was not a contract between equals. Based on His undeserving love for all of humanity, God chose to make a promise—that He himself guaranteed—with someone He had created. God made the covenant with faithful Abraham, and its benefits carry all the way down to our present day, for all who choose to enter into a relationship of love and obedience with the God of the universe.

CHAPTER *2*

A Promise-Making God

by Stephen Lennox

ROBERT WILLIAM SERVICE'S POEM "The Cremation of Sam McGee" tells the story of a promise. Sam McGee, who never felt warm after going to the Arctic from Tennessee, makes his companion promise to cremate his remains after he dies. Sure enough, after a long dogsled ride through the bitterly cold terrain, McGee passes on. The companion, having given his word, must haul around the corpse until he can keep his promise. As much as he would have liked to dump the body and move on without the added weight, he feels bound to honor his word. "After all," he observes, "a promise made is a debt unpaid." Finally, having found fuel enough to carry out his promise, he "burrowed a hole in the glowing coal" and "stuffed in Sam McGee." When he finally worked up the courage to look in and see what remained of the body, he found—

> Sam, looking cool and calm,
> In the heart of the furnace roar;
> And he wore a smile you could see a mile,
> And he said: "Please close that door.
> It's fine in here, but I greatly fear
> You'll let in the cold and storm—
> Since I left Plumtree down in Tennessee,
> It's the first time I've been warm."

21

From this humorous ballad comes the important truth that "a promise made is a debt unpaid," a debt to be satisfied at any cost. In the Bible, we find that God takes His promises seriously, satisfying each one. Whether it was His promise to rescue His people from Egypt, to satisfy their physical needs, to protect them from danger, or to bring the Messiah, God always kept His word.

While there is much to be said about God the Promise Keeper, we ought to recognize the profound implications of the fact that God makes promises at all. Genesis 15 describes several important divine promises. After exploring this passage in some detail, we will see what we can learn about a God who makes promises.

The World of Genesis 15

From the opening chapters of Genesis, it is clear that creation had a problem. The world that God created as good had become terribly bad. Sin, having taken root in the first parents, spread like a cancer, corrupting the whole world and all its inhabitants. Even after Noah, the world continued its downward spiral of sin. Most distressing to the divine heart was how sin had broken the relationship between God and His people.

God set about to reconcile the world to himself in a most unusual fashion. He called one man, Abram (later named Abraham), to leave his own people and become the forefather of the nation of Israel. Through this nation, God promised to bless all nations of the earth (Genesis 12). God revealed how He intended to bless the earth and reconcile it to himself in the centuries to follow. Through the Jewish nation, He produced the Messiah. Paul described God's plan this way: "God was reconciling the world to himself in Christ" (2 Corinthians 5:19).

For whatever reasons, God did not execute His plan quickly. Instead, Abraham's call was followed by long periods of divine silence. Abraham, meanwhile, experienced one embarrassing and difficult experience after another. First, he was evicted from Egypt (Genesis 12:10-20), then territorial disputes forced a separation from his own nephew (Genesis 13:1-18). After this, Abraham became embroiled in the middle of a conflict between warring cities (Genesis 14:1-24).

Genesis 15 marks an important moment in these early days of God's plan. In this chapter God unfolds more fully how He intends to reconcile the world to himself. He reveals something of that plan to Abraham in the form of two promises (covenants): (1) Abraham would father a son, and (2) his descendants would inherit the land of Canaan. How those promises fit into God's plan and the surprising way that God committed himself to them deserves a closer look.

The chapter opens with God appearing to Abraham in a vision and identifying himself as Abraham's "shield" and "very great reward" (v. 1). Although "shield" usually implies protection, here it means more. The Hebrew word can be translated "king"; this is probably what fits best here. By revealing himself as Abraham's king, God challenged Abraham to full obedience. He must follow God as a loyal subject, obeying each step in the divine plan. How well Abraham followed God was evident on Mount Moriah when he was willing to offer Isaac as a sacrifice. God's introduction as Abraham's king also brought a message of reassurance with its reminder that Abraham is not traveling this strange road alone. He is in the service of his Sovereign.

To understand what God meant by His reference to "great reward," we must return to Genesis 14. There, in verses 22-24, Abraham refused to accept a reward from the king of Sodom. The reward was rightfully his because of his military help. Abraham, however, refused to accept any payment from this king, choosing instead to wait for his reward from God. He preferred the invisible riches of God's kingdom to the visible wealth of the king of Sodom. Genesis 15:1 reveals what a wise choice this was, for God promised him a "very great reward." Still more encouraging for Abraham, this reward was to be found, not in what God gives, but in God himself: "I am . . . your very great reward." It is always a wise bargain to choose an invisible God over anything visible.

A Question and a Promise

God's identification of himself as Abraham's reward raised a question in Abraham's mind, a question that prompts his comments in verses 2-3. While he knew that in having God he had all things, Abraham was troubled by the fact that he had no son. When he died, his considerable wealth would go to his chief servant, Eliezer, according to the custom of that day. In a complaint that reveals both Abraham's confidence and submission to God ("Sovereign LORD"), he reminds God that he has no son of his own.

God responds to this complaint in the form of a solemn promise. Abraham would not leave his wealth to his servant. Instead, he would become a father, and his own son would be his heir. God sweetens this promise still more by promising that this son would be the first of many descendants. Just how many dawned on Abraham as he stood beneath the clear night sky of Canaan and gazed up into the uncountable stars. In that day, the promise of a son and countless descendants was the best news a childless old man could hear.

As incredible as this promise was, Abraham believed that God would do just what He promised. Centuries later, Paul applauded Abraham's faith. He described it as "being fully persuaded that God had power to do what he had promised" (Romans 4:21). Such a leap of faith was nothing new for Abraham. He had believed enough to leave his home and follow God, not knowing where he was going (Hebrews 11:8). Later when God asked him to surrender his most precious possession—this same promised son—

he obeyed without waiting for answers to his questions. Faith so characterized his life that he became known as "the father of all who believe" (Romans 4:11). When God saw that Abraham took Him at His word, He "credited [it] to him as righteousness" (Romans 4:9). God recognized Abraham's great faith and was very pleased with it.

Perhaps to express His pleasure, God revealed himself still further to Abraham in Genesis 15:7. This time He described himself as the Lord who had taken Abraham from his home in Ur to possess the land of Canaan. As in verse 2, Abraham responded to God's word with a question, "How can I know [for sure]?" (v. 8). How surprising that only two verses after being commended for his faith, Abraham questions God! This question arose, however, not from Abraham's lack of faith, but because his faith needed strengthening.

Some people question God in order to avoid His demands upon their lives. Like the lawyer who resisted Jesus' call to love his neighbor (Luke 10:25-37), they throw out questions like smoke screens, hoping to hide their lack of obedience. This was not Abraham's motivation. He already had faith; he wanted that faith strengthened. His question sprang from the same motivation as the request of the man in Mark 9:24: "I do believe; help me overcome my unbelief!" God does not mind our questions, if they are asked to strengthen faith.

Sealing the Deal

That God did not mind Abraham's question is evident from Genesis 15:9-21, where God provides the certainty Abraham sought. As in verse 5, this certainty came through an object lesson. Earlier it was a starry night sky; here the certainty came through a bloody ceremony. God instructed Abraham to take several animals and birds, cut the animals in half, and lay them opposite each other in the open field. (He did not cut up the birds, perhaps because they were too small.) Today we finalize contracts in a lawyer's office at a table piled high with legal documents that the average person could not begin to understand. Abraham would be as baffled by our modern "ceremonies" as we are by the legal ceremony described in these verses. In order to seal a promise, one of the parties would walk between the dismembered pieces. In effect, he would be saying, "Let what happened to these animals happen to me if I break my word."

After carrying out his instructions to cut up the animals, Abraham waited for God to act. We don't know how long he waited, but it must have been long enough for buzzards to get wind of the carcasses and descend for dinner. Apparently unaware of the cause for the divine delay, Abraham chased them off and continued to wait. Finally, around sunset, he fell into a deep, unnatural, and unsettling sleep. He felt himself immersed in terrifying darkness. Then out of that darkness, he heard God solemnly promise to give the land of Canaan to Abraham's descendants. There would be some delay (400 years) and some difficulty (the darkness of slavery and mistreatment), but the light of God's favor would shine again, bringing the Israelites into the Promised Land. Abraham, meanwhile, would die in peace at an old age.

In one of the most striking pictures in the Bible, a blazing torch and a pot filled with fire and smoke passed between the animal carcasses, unassisted by any visible means. These objects were chosen, I suspect, to reveal something of the divine character. As a torch lights up the darkness, God reveals His nature to humanity. As a flame consumes what is temporary, the unworthy elements of our existence—the "wood, hay, or straw" (1 Corinthians 3:12)—are consumed by His greatness. The "smoking firepot" reminds us that a full understanding of God is hidden behind the smoke of His mystery. As these objects passed between the animal pieces, God willingly committed himself to keep His promises to Abraham. God himself passed between the pieces in a solemn promise to Abraham.

Biblical history reveals that God did, in fact, keep His word. He gave Abraham a son, Isaac, who became the father of Jacob. Jacob (also known as Israel) had 12 sons from whom the 12 tribes of Israel trace their descent. Just as God promised, Abraham's descendants grew until they outnumbered the stars in the sky. After four centuries of slavery in Egypt, Moses liberated the Israelites, leaving behind a plundered and defeated Egypt. They entered the Promised Land under Joshua and defeated the Canaanites with God's assistance. Abraham, as predicted, died in peace and prosperity at the ripe, old age of 175 (Genesis 25:7-8). How wonderfully reassuring to remember that God is the original Promise Keeper!

God the Promise-Maker

The emphasis of Genesis 15 is not on how God keeps His promises, however, but on the fact that He is even willing to make promises. Throughout the Bible we find that God is always making promises to His people. He promises to answer their prayers, comfort the bereaved, guide the searching, pardon the guilty, protect the endangered, enlighten the simple, provide for the needy, and much more. Over and over we meet a God who willingly "[walks] between the pieces" for His people. Clearly, not all of the Bible's promises are meant for us to claim. God's promise to provide a son was given to Abraham, not every childless couple. How then should Christians read the promises in the Bible? They should ask first what they can learn about a God who makes promises.

One thing to be noted is that God's promises imply a divine plan. If I promise my children that on a certain day we will drive to visit their grandparents, it is only after I have made a plan. I have consulted our work and school schedules, found a time when there are no other pressing commitments, and made certain the car can handle the trip. To make such a promise without having a plan would be irresponsible (not to mention terribly disappointing to my children). It would be like the man Jesus spoke about who built a tower without counting the cost. These promises to Abraham clearly imply that God already had a plan, a plan that included Isaac and the land of Canaan.

We also see this was no ordinary plan. God's promise in verse 4 strongly emphasizes that the one born to Abraham, not Eliezer, will inherit everything. The Hebrew words of verse 13 are quite emphatic: "know for certain." We also see the importance of God's plan in the ceremony of verses 9-21. It is so important that God himself "[walks] between the pieces" to guarantee that it will come about. Abraham may not have understood the full importance of this plan or when God would fulfill it, but history has made it plain to us. God's plan was nothing less than His way of reconciling the world to himself and solving the problem that sin had created. All who have found salvation in Christ are part of that great plan and can rejoice that they follow a promise-making God.

Second, since God makes promises, He must place a high premium on faith. A promise, by definition, implies that the fulfillment remains in the future. It is too late to promise a trip to Grandma's house when we are pulling into her driveway. By that time, no promise is necessary. The waiting that comes between promise and fulfillment is not easy, however. Only faith in the promise-maker enables one to endure the delay. God's promises are an important way that He builds faith into His people. How often in times of struggle and testing have I wished God would immediately intervene and fulfill His promises. If the answer were to come immediately, however, I could not develop the faith that He values so highly.

Why does God consider faith so important? According to the writer of Hebrews, only those with faith are able "to please God" (11:6). But why is this so? What is there about God that makes faith the only way to delight His heart? Hebrews 11:6 goes on to say that faith is necessary "because anyone who comes to [God] must believe that he exists and that he rewards those who earnestly seek him." Only by faith can we access a God who belongs to a realm not reached by human reason. Only by faith can we understand that God wants to be found, is fair enough to reward our best efforts, and knows who "earnestly" seek Him. Only by faith can we understand what God wants from us; only by faith can we meet His expectations. In other words, faith is essential to know God's existence, His nature, and His will. If faith makes this possible, no wonder God makes such a special point of building it into our lives through His promises.

Finally, in His habit of promise making, God reveals His love for us. When is the last time you promised something to a total stranger? You only make promises to those with whom you already have some relationship. God's promises prove the reality of the relationships He has willingly initiated with His people. God did not have to make any promises to Abraham. His sole motivation was love for Abraham and for people in general. All of God's promises have arisen from a heart of love and compassion.

Why, after all, does God make promises? He does not make promises to serve His needs as if His ego needed the boost that would come from seeing our delighted reaction. Nor does God need to make promises in order for His plans to succeed. He could easily have given a son to Abraham and Sarah without telling them about it first. He makes promises for our benefit, not His. He makes promises because He cares enough to become a debtor to us. After all, "a promise made is a debt unpaid." God made the promises in Genesis 15 because He cared about Abraham. He knew how difficult it was to wait for God. He knew how hard it was to understand delay and unanswered questions. It was love for Abraham that made God "pass between the pieces."

Conclusion

When we promise our children something we know they have been longing for and something we know we can deliver, are we not looking primarily for the delight that our promise will bring? Why do we want to delight them if not because we love them? At times Christians struggle with feelings of loneliness and discouragement. Problems loom before us like mountains, and the deep darkness of an uncertain future hides our path. God seems so distant as our prayers go unanswered. At times like this, God's promises remind us that He is willing to "pass between the pieces" for His people. He knows our struggles with delay, and He lovingly provides through His promises a bench on which to rest while we wait.

While we are right to celebrate a promise-*keeping* God, we can also rejoice in a God who *makes* promises. His promises show that He is a God with an important plan, a plan that means salvation for all. He is a God who longs to cultivate faith in His people, knowing that we need faith to follow Him. A God who makes promises shows that He loves people enough to "pass between the pieces" for them.

About the author: Stephen Lennox, Ph.D., is assistant professor of religion at Indiana Wesleyan University, Marion, Indiana.

Deuteronomy 6

INTRODUCTION

The Book of Deuteronomy is a warm and personal sermon in which Moses warns the people against disobedience and urges them to walk according to God's will. The events described in Deuteronomy occur right on the threshold of a major change for the Israelites. The period of Moses' leadership is about to end, and they are on the edge of moving into the Promised Land.

Upon his departure, Moses is trying to impress upon the people that the events in the past have been God's way of leading them to His goal for them. However, they must understand that reaching that goal depends on their commitment and obedience to God.

In chapter 6 of Deuteronomy, we are introduced to the most basic belief of the Old Testament. In what is referred to as the Shema, the Israelites are reminded that God is one, unlike the many gods of other cultures. He is not merely the first or most important God among many gods. He is the one and only God, who is all-powerful. This truth is so important, Moses instructs them to teach it to their children, talk about it at home, put it on their hands and foreheads, and attach it to the doors of their homes. We still find the Hebrew people following these commands when we see a mezuzah on the doorpost of a Jewish home today.

The truth of the words "The LORD our God, the LORD is one" (6:4) is still important to all Christians today. The One who led Israel from slavery in Egypt to freedom in the Promised Land is the same One who brings us salvation from the slavery of sin. We need to hear the words of the Shema and listen to this part of our salvation history.

CHAPTER *3*

Remembering the One True God's Faithful Love

by Melanie Starks Kierstead

MY FRIEND CHRIS AMAZES ME! He has a memory for names and detail that I have seldom seen in anyone else. Chris is a Bible scholar who remembers and relates God's principles and illustrations. He also has a heart for God and a call to preach. This combination makes for some excellent sermon illustrations where he cites first and last names as well as the details that clarify the truth he is trying to make. For some people, making tedious notes would be necessary as well as hearing the illustrations and details repeatedly in order to remember them. For others who have never heard the story or principles, through Chris's communicating genius, they can see for the first time the teachings of God's Word.

Although Moses claimed that he was not much of an orator and therefore wouldn't be much good as a leader, the speeches in Deuteronomy betray his excellence in communication skills. We find passages from his speeches in Deuteronomy quoted in the New Testament many times and by Jesus himself repeatedly.

In Deuteronomy 6 a new generation heard God's law.

The people of Israel had been wandering in the wilderness for decades, and all but a couple of the original adult Israelites who left Egypt together had died. After spying in the land 40 years before, the people of Israel had fled the Canaanite border, terrified at the prospects of invading that pagan nation that seemed so advanced. God refused to let any of the cowardly doubters enter the land of Canaan, and over the next 40 years, they died. Now, in preparation for taking Canaan, the elderly Moses was again sharing the law that God had revealed to him on Mount Sinai—this time with the children of those who had heard it before. Details and incidents from Israel's past, as well as commandments and underlying precepts, were presented to the people of Israel. Moses urged them, with the wisdom of his years, to prepare to meet the challenge of God's mission for them so that they might reflect His glory. Just as he knew God and God's work, he clearly knew what would be required of the people of Israel in order for them to enjoy the promises of God in their new land. His experience with God had taught him that total obedience and undivided allegiance would demonstrate the love that God deserved and expected in response to His gracious favor.

Moses called the people of Israel together saying, "Hear, O Israel!" The single, most-recited scripture by Jews is this passage, which they call the Shema, the Hebrew word translated "hear." This passage (vv. 4-9), in conjunction with a couple others, has been a daily prayer for the Jewish people for millennia. It is a call to remember who and what their God is as well as to carefully remember His commandments. Jesus, like the Jews of His day, added a commandment from Leviticus 19:18, "Love your neighbor as yourself." The act of loving God cannot be complete without a demonstrated love for those around the believer as well.

In this passage, a threefold message unfolds: (1) The Lord alone is our God. (2) The Lord is to be loved completely. (3) This must be remembered by all means necessary. A description of how these people might constantly remind themselves of God's law follows this strong pronouncement. Moses calls his people to *hear* once again (or some for the first time) the details of their covenant with the one God.

Our God Is Loved Through Obedience

Although the law of Moses is constructed in treaty form like many ancient law codes, such as the code of Hammurabi, there is a distinct difference. Love is seldom, if ever, expected between participants in the ancient covenants. This covenant is between God, who loves His people, and His people, who, in return, love Him. Obedience to the precepts of God is rooted in love for Him. Indeed, Jesus said that the way to identify those who love God is to observe those who obey Him (see John 14:15).

Chapter 6 of Deuteronomy deals with the commandment of God to love Him and Him alone. This Mosaic summary (v. 5) is essentially a positive restatement of the first of the Ten Commandments. The promise that comes with obedience is the continued blessing of God on the Israelites even in generations to come (vv. 2-3). Moses taught that they were to love only this God, not to mingle their affection for Him with that for other gods or objects of interest.

Before the people of Israel would be able to conquer the Canaanite land, their focus had to be set clearly on a single object of affection—Yahweh. They would fail unless their sights were set on establishing a nation that would follow God alone. Moses knew that what Canaan had to offer would be pretty enticing after their wilderness wanderings. He knew that most of them could not even remember the splendors that he himself knew from Israel's days in Egypt. They dare not be distracted! They must be single-minded in the conquering of Canaan. If they were seduced by the wealth, amazed by the culture of Canaan, deterred by the flowing streams after their desert days, or if their imaginations were sparked by the enchanting gods of the Canaanites, they would never be able to have the land that God had promised to their forefather Abraham. Moses reminded them that Yahweh was their only God, the only object of their worship, admiration, and loyalty.

Obedience Comes by Remembering

Obedient love of God comes through being fully aware of the provisions of God and His law. The commandments of God were to be taken to heart, so to speak. The law was to be the constant subject of thought and conversation. They were to teach the children to follow the commandments. They were to talk about the provisions and commandments throughout the day, at home, in their travels, at bedtime, and at dawn. In other words, everywhere and always would be just enough to serve God. His provisions and commandments were to be bound on their hands and foreheads and posted on the doorposts and gates of their homes. The Jewish people responded by literally strapping little boxes with key scriptures to their heads and forearms. They built into their doorposts and gateways little pockets where they kept containers of scripture. They did this in order to surround themselves with reminders of the faithfulness as well as the commandments of their God.

Heart and Soul and Strength

One command summed up the entire teaching of God: "Love the LORD your God with all your heart and with all your soul and with all your strength" (Deuteronomy 6:5). Jesus quoted this in three Gospel accounts and called it the "greatest commandment" in Matthew 22:38.

Because the New Testament was written to a Greek audience (as compared to the Old Testament Hebrew audience), Matthew, Mark, and Luke incorporated "mind" into this commandment. This emphasizes that every aspect of our being must be fully committed to the mission of the one true God.

Passing on the Message of God's Faithfulness

Israelite children were to be taught the marvelous story of God's redeeming acts, which is the background and basis of the law. Moses encouraged the people to be ready to answer their children's questions with the story of their parents' deliverance from Egyptian bondage, thus connecting generations of those who were honored by God with His loving protection.

Some parents today encourage their children to be free thinkers, independent to choose which religion they will follow, if any. In fact, many people mix and match their religious facts, creating the god that most reflects themselves. A Wesleyan concept of living a holy life, a cleansing breath of Zen Buddhism, a little bit of the Calvinistic sovereignty of God, an exercise class in tai chi, and a Navajo dream catcher for good luck—there we have it: a "spiritual person." We have gone a long way from frontlets worn around Jewish heads, fragments of scriptures bound to the hands, and constant conversation about God's goodness and expectations. Yet it was precisely this focus on God and the terror of mixing foreign elements into their understanding of their Provider that kept Israel's religion pure.

God has revealed himself to His people. As God, He is the only eternal One. He is the God who loves and provides. Just as God reveals himself to His people, God expects His people to respond to Him with love and obedient service. We also have a responsibility to keep our God ever before us by identifying His faithfulness in history and following His commandments in the present. God's truth must govern our homes. To do that, the truth must be evident and enforced.

Moses acted like a coach preparing a team likely headed to the championship game. At the end of the regular season, the team is psyched and confident. The coach demands that they focus. They think that they are ready. However the coach has final words of instruction because he has something they don't have—a sense of history and a clear sense of mission.

Moses knew something else. He realized he would not accompany them and they would have to be ready to carry on without him. Their understanding of the foundational principles and unchangeable commandments would alone hold them true to the glorious faith of their father Abraham and to the gracious favor God had bestowed on the descendants of Abraham. Absolutely necessary for Moses' people was a focus to conquer as well as a focus to live a life worthy of their calling. Like a team headed into the championship, they assumed they were ready, but a great coach now calls them aside with words of instruction. He urges them to remember their basic skills, their usual plays, and the power that has brought them this far. He insists that they reflect on their teamwork and the essence of their mission. Each member must prepare individually to meet the challenge with a single-minded focus on the goal. In a pep talk, he speaks from years of experience and commands his players to focus, focus, focus!

Rewards

The immediate fulfillment of God's promise would be that of material wealth in the form of natural resources (v. 3), and cities, houses, wells, and gardens built by the hands of their enemies (vv. 10-11). In all they would do, the Israelites were to remember the loving works of God—day and night, from season to season, while tilling the land and enjoying the spoils of Canaan. They were to regard each day as a loving gift from God and to respond to Him with loving obedience, with their whole heart, soul, and might.

Conclusion

We humans forget so easily! Without Moses' recorded words in Deuteronomy, Israel was in danger of forgetting. Forgetting how God's mercy had delivered them from slavery. Forgetting the good things that they were about to possess at the end of their wilderness wanderings. God sent Moses along to remind them of where they had been and where they were going—as well as who made it all possible.

Today we as Christians are just as prone to forget the God we love. We forget how great and majestic God is when we get so caught up in the mundane events of this world. We forget how dependent we are on God's provision and mercy when we seem to have all that we need—and more—from our own efforts.

Thankfully, God sends persons to us like my friend Chris—persons who remember the details of God's story and remind us in a thousand little ways that we are to love God with all our heart, soul, and strength. Thank God for all the reminders like Moses and Chris that He sends our way!

About the author: Melanie Starks Kierstead, Ph.D., is campus pastor and professor of religion and philosophy at Bartlesville Wesleyan College, Bartlesville, Oklahoma.

Jeremiah 31:31-34

INTRODUCTION

Jeremiah was a visible and vocal prophet in Israel for 40 years. He prophesied during a time of turmoil among Egypt, Assyria, and Babylon—the "superpowers" of those days. From 626 B.C. until 586 B.C. he warned the Hebrews about impending defeat .

Jeremiah has been called the weeping prophet because of his style of expression in the two books of the Bible attributed to him—Jeremiah and Lamentations. He not only carried a burden for the sinning Israelites, but felt their pain as well. He preached that the judgment of God was going to come on them for their sin. However, he also was careful to point out that repentance, if sincere, would postpone the inevitable doom. The people did not heed Jeremiah's message, and they suffered a humiliating exile in Babylon.

Jeremiah was not a popular prophet (were any?). The people and the king tried to stop his message. Once some men threw him down a dry well in an attempt to silence him. He used the experience to warn Israel about being "cracked cisterns" that let God's love seep away. Another time, he dictated the words of his message to his secretary, Baruch, and sent the prophecy to the king. The king ripped the scroll into little pieces with a knife and threw the whole book into the fire. Undaunted, Jeremiah dictated the entire message again.

The words recorded in Jeremiah 31:31-34 make Jeremiah a unique part of our story of salvation. Jeremiah cites a "new" covenant that God is going to make with humans, a covenant that God would write on the hearts of individual men and women. Jeremiah's words are the only reference to the new covenant in the Old Testament, yet they represent one of the deepest insights of the entire Old Testament. This covenant pointed toward a time when saving knowledge of God would be available apart from the sacrificial system of the Jews. It pointed toward the time of the Christian era—our time—when persons who confess in their hearts Jesus as Lord make up the Church.

Jeremiah's message about the new covenant was important groundwork laid for the salvation that was to come in Jesus. With it, God paved the way for a "heart relationship" with Him.

CHAPTER 4

The Law on Our Hearts

by Clair Allen Budd

THE NEWS RUMBLED LIKE AN earthquake across the state. Dave*, a young pastor from a neighboring church, had abandoned his wife and children for the church-office secretary. *How could this happen?* I wondered alone and with colleagues. *How does a leader in the church who had preached the principles of God break with all moral decency like this?*

I realized it had not occurred suddenly. Certainly Dave's actions seemed sudden to those who heard the news. Yet the relationship that Dave and the secretary were "announcing" had been developing for months. During that time, he probably disciplined his children, paid bills, made household repairs, and fed the dog. He lived with his wife and perhaps even followed society's standards of being a good husband. He may have even showered her with flowers and kisses from time to time.

His behavior maintained an appearance of appropriateness, but his affection had begun to drift. The marriage vows he so boldly professed a few years before possessed no power to hold his heart at home.

A Better Way

A similar situation formed the background for Jeremiah's prophecy about the new covenant. "I will put my law

41

within them, and I will write it on their hearts" (31:33, NRSV). Without a doubt, Jeremiah's prophecy suggests that the existing covenant was inadequate. If it had been adequate, there would have been no need for revision, let alone replacement. We should not speak about the covenant as flawed, however, because Jeremiah is clear: The fundamental flaw was the failure of the people of Israel to live within the covenant provisions. "It will not be like the covenant I made with their forefathers . . . because they broke [it]" (v. 32).

During the period leading up to Jeremiah's ministry, the Israelites had begun yielding to pressure from surrounding nations to worship gods other than the God of Abraham and Isaac. The nation had lived under the military and political power of Assyria. They had also accepted and practiced the worship of Assyrian deities, in part as a way of avoiding further military conquest and economic devastation. That is, their religious compromises may have been a matter of expediency rather than conviction.

Interestingly, they did not abandon worship of God. They worshiped the God of their fathers alongside the foreign gods. They might even have argued, "We are keeping the provisions of the covenant; we still worship God and sacrifice to Him as the law demands."

Yet while seeming in their own eyes to keep the letter of the law, they missed the spirit of it. The spirit of the covenant called for worship of God *only;* while their worship was of God *and* _____. You can fill in the blank with any number of things, such as political independence, societal respectability, material prosperity. In reality, they weren't keeping the letter of the law either. When single-hearted loyalty to God fades, righteous conduct becomes less clear and courageous. In the case of the Israelites, even child sacrifice had become a part of their worship, though it was specifically forbidden in the covenant (Jeremiah

7:31). Their disobedience and falling away were obvious to all but themselves.

Keeping the Law

Under the old covenant, the Israelites developed a strictly legal understanding of religion. Religion was mostly a matter of what persons do, that is, the rules they keep. If all the rules were kept, individuals were free to do whatever they liked with the rest of their time, energy, and resources.

Sometimes we call this legal understanding of the covenant the deuteronomic code because the Book of Deuteronomy specifies blessings for obeying certain provisions of the law and curses for disobeying certain other provisions. Deuteronomy 30:15-20 summarizes this idea.

Most of us develop this understanding of religion as we are growing up. I remember thinking as a child that I must be in favor with God because I had fulfilled God's command of "not forsaking the assembling . . . together" (Hebrews 10:25, KJV) by attending church every week. In fact, I attended weekly Sunday School, Sunday worship, a youth service, an evangelistic service, *and* a prayer meeting.

Of course, my Christian parents compelled me to do so. However that doesn't matter because the focus in this understanding of religion is on outward conduct. The flaw in understanding the covenant in this way is that we think we can begin accumulating "credits" that we can redeem as needed. Some students at the Christian college I attended had sophisticated systems for this. They thought they could redeem their "credit" for not missing church services the previous three weeks by attending a movie (a violation of college rules).

The person with a religion that focuses on outward conduct and rule keeping can always find a legal loophole for doing what he or she wants. I remember seeing a cartoon several years ago that captured this attitude of rebellion while maintaining technical compliance. A little boy sat on his childsize rocker, holding his teddy bear and facing an empty corner of the room. Looking over his shoulder, he uttered these defiant words: "I may be sitting down on the outside, but I'm standing up on the inside." Fortunately, the religion God requires is not one we can manipulate in this way, because it focuses first on the person's *inner* being, not merely the outer conduct.

It isn't that the law is unimportant or can be ignored. The old covenant was God's plan for that time and was in place to help the people of Israel relate properly to God. The people had reduced God's plan to a system of religious rules. Jesus reaffirmed a proper perspective when He said that He had come to fulfill, not replace, the law (see Matthew 5:17). He introduced a new way of relating to God, yet one that was and is entirely consistent with what the Israelites already had known of God through the law. (See Hebrews 8—11 for a fuller discussion of this idea.)

We recognize easily that the law points out our failures and shortcomings (see Romans 7:7-13). When the line between right and wrong is illuminated, the sharp focus easily shows how we moved to the wrong side of the road. We may have a variety of emotions about the experience of crossing the line, but God's standard of holy living is the same for every person. The law is the high beam that helps us see which side of the line we are on.

Jeremiah saw that the law, while it could point the way and illuminate the road, could not steer the car. The law *calls* us to a higher place in our relationship with God, but it does not (and cannot) *cause* it to happen.

New and Improved

Advertising agencies seem to believe that most consumers are drawn to a new product or a new version of an older product. Try counting the number of labels in the grocery store that contain the words *new* or *improved*. I sometimes wonder what the flaw was in the older version of a product that required it to be fixed?

Jeremiah struggled with that idea in relationship to the covenant. As we have seen, the old covenant played a particular role that God had in mind for that period of time. The old covenant wasn't flawed. It didn't need to be fixed; it needed to be retired.

So Jeremiah, under the inspiration of the Holy Spirit, introduced the new covenant that God intended to enter with His people. Note that this was not a covenant that God initiated in Jeremiah's day. The verbs are all in the future tense. Centuries later, the new covenant found its beginning and its fulfillment in the life, death, and resurrection of Jesus Christ. Through faith in His perfect obedience to God, most clearly revealed in His sacrificial death, we can share in all the blessings of the new covenant.

We might ask, "What is *new* about the new covenant? How is it different?"

Relational Religion

Religion understood as rule keeping is quite impersonal. Rules possess no personality, and rule breakers often view rule enforcers as adversaries. Many people today, as well as in Jeremiah's day, view God as some sort of cosmic police officer. Obedience may issue out of fear, but many people simply rebel against this view of a harsh, anxious-to-punish God.

In Jeremiah's new covenant we discover a new focus on personal religion. The person and character of God come center stage with His prophecy that "they will all know me" (v. 34). Jesus responded to challenges from His contemporaries to show them the Father by saying that if they had seen Him, they *had* seen the Father (see John 14:9). The writer to the Hebrews perhaps captures this best: "In the past God spoke to our forefathers through the prophets at many times and in various ways, but in these last days he has spoken to us by his Son, whom he appointed heir of all things, and through whom he made the universe. *The Son is the radiance of God's glory and the exact representation of his being"* (1:1-3, emphasis added).

What we see of God when we look into the face of Jesus is His great love for us. Love sends His Son to die for our transgressions (see John 3:16). Love reaches out to make peace when we are full of animosity and hostility (see Romans 5:10). It is love from beginning to end.

Love is not a characteristic of laws and punishment, judges and justice. Love *is* a characteristic of personal relationships, and it's this kind of personal relationship that Jeremiah is revealing to the people of his day. It is a relationship where God and people will belong to each other in trust, intimacy, and faithfulness.

The new covenant promises to provide the basis for this new relationship. God will forgive their iniquity (that is, their sin) (v. 34). The people cannot rectify their wrongs. However, this God of love, who will enter into relationship with them and be known by them, can—and will—cover their sin so that it cannot be seen or held against them again.

Inner Religion

We have seen that the people of Israel came to understand the old covenant as a code of outward compliance to an external, impersonal law. In the new covenant, God promises to make His law internal. He's looking not only for public righteousness but also for an obedience that comes out of the core of the person.

I think I understand this best as a parent of three children. My wife and I work hard to provide a home environment that will help our kids grow into mature, responsible Christian adults. Part of this means establishing standards and guidelines for conduct, both positive and negative.

Often we see evidence of the external law at work. Our 10-year-old son, until recently, cleaned his room because it was an obligation he had to fulfill to receive his allowance or to invite a friend over for the night. I doubted that the behavior would continue for long if the "parent police" weren't present to provide the appropriate payoffs or sanctions. However, we worked, hoped, and prayed that at some point he would keep his room clean because he appreciated the value of living in a clean, uncluttered environment. We're excited that we are seeing signs that this "law" is becoming a part of him.

Certainly some issues are much more important than whether one's room is clean—such as issues of morality and eternity. The idea holds true, however: God's intent with the new covenant is to place the law *within* us so that it is something we "buy into" out of principle and align ourselves with through choice rather than outside coercion or sense of duty.

The nature of law is different in the new covenant as well, though Jeremiah only hints at it here. Ezekiel, one of Jeremiah's contemporaries, calls this a "new spirit" that God will place within people (Ezekiel 36:26). The law or spirit that God graciously places within us is the law of love: love guiding every attitude and action, directing our entire person toward the welfare of others and the glory of God.

I've often heard that we can't legislate morality. The government can pass laws in an effort to cause or inhibit various kinds of behavior. Yet only God can touch the inner wellspring of a person to produce morality.

Loyal Religion

This focus on the inner person draws attention to the heart (see Jeremiah 31:33). We recognize that God was not referring to the physical organ that supplies blood to the body. Rather, the people of Jeremiah's day understood this symbolism to represent the valuing, choosing center of a person. Obedience to a law or standard of conduct becomes far easier and more natural when the heart motivates a person to do so.

What broke God's heart about the Israelites breaking the covenant was not so much the particular violations as it was the disloyalty and distrust of which the violations were symptoms. The glorious reality of the new, revitalized covenant is that God can create within the human heart a single-mindedness and a loyalty to Him, in addition to providing forgiveness of sins and blessing every area of life.

The apostle Paul sees this, I believe, when he writes to the Philippians, "Work out your salvation with fear and trembling, for it is God who works in you to will and to act according to his good purpose" (2:12-13).

Worship of the one true God, the living God, must be undivided and wholehearted (that is, holy). Such worship begins in the heart as unwavering loyalty to God and then plays out into every sphere and activity of life. The new covenant makes it clear that such integrity and consistency only come through God's initiative to transform us by placing His own law within our hearts.

Unfortunately, some Christians believe that such transformation will remove them from the plane of human suffering. The people in Jeremiah's day believed that God would protect them from military defeat simply because they were the people of God. As Jesus articulates the new covenant, He makes it clear that rain falls on the righteous as well as the unrighteous (Matthew 5:45) and that pain and sorrow are not necessarily direct results of sin in one's life.

Weakness and frailty characterize mortal life. Pain and tragedy come to all, regardless of spiritual state. Yet the heart where God has placed His law will avoid much pain, because the righteousness that flows from the person will be a protection from much self-induced sorrow.

Before a couple in our church adopted him, Jon* was an abused child. He struggled with many issues, including low self-esteem, tense personal relationships, fights, and poor grades at school. People pointed out his shortcomings, and he tried to do better but without success.

Jon's eyes were opened to the God of the new covenant at a summer youth camp, and he opened his heart to His transforming work. It was an emotional night as Jon struggled with the implications of letting God be his first and only allegiance. Yet his face radiated with joy when he stood and testified how God had touched him that night.

Jon still struggled with the memories of early rejection and abuse. He still fought low self-esteem and had difficulty with schoolwork. However, he quit fighting at school and began learning how to treat other people with respect because God had put a new law of love deep within his being.

Like Jon, we can try to live up to the demands of God's law. The Pharisees in Jesus' day had developed an elaborate system to help them achieve this goal. Yet Jesus chastised them for being "whitewashed tombs" (Matthew 23:27). Or we can, like the Israelites of Jeremiah's day, allow loyalty to other things to divert us from the purity God demands.

We will find that obedience by law evades our reach. God's nature demands wholehearted allegiance, not behavioral compliance alone. Such allegiance is not natural to us because of the stain of Adam's sin with which we were all born. Still, God promises to bring about the inner change required, to write His law upon our hearts. This is God's promise of the new covenant—a promise with all the potential of the cross of Christ and all the power of His blood to deal redemptively with our sin and disloyalty.

---

*Name has been changed.

About the author: Clair Allen Budd, Ph.D., enjoys playing at golf when he's not teaching Christian ministries at Asbury College near Lexington, Kentucky.

Psalm 23

INTRODUCTION

Among all the great and inspiring writings in the Bible, perhaps the Book of Psalms stands out as most unique in its beauty and variety. Psalms covers the full range of human emotions from the lowest cries of despair to the highest praise of the Almighty. We use the wide variety contained in the Psalms in many ways—as songs, prayers, and inspirational pieces. Most Bible scholars identify eight different categories of psalms: personal, penitential, praise, prayer, messianic, historical, liturgical, and ones that attribute power and majesty to God.

The Hebrew name for the Book of Psalms means "the Book of Praises." Ancient Hebrews used the Psalms liturgically, and the practice continues today by both Jews and Christians. Many of the great historical leaders of the Church have had high praise for the Psalms. Martin Luther said that the Psalter "might well be called a little Bible. In it is comprehended most beautifully and briefly everything that is in the entire Bible." John Calvin said about the Book of Psalms, "there is nothing wanting which relates to the knowledge of eternal salvation." Dietrich Bonhoeffer wrote, "The Psalter occupies a unique place in the Holy Scriptures. It is God's Word and, with a few exceptions, the prayer of men as well."*

The Psalms were collected over several centuries. The final compiling was finished around 200 B.C. The songs and prayers flowed through the pens of several authors, including David, Solomon, Asaph, Moses, and others whose names are lost to us.

Psalm 23 is the most well-known and most-beloved psalm. We memorize it. We decorate our walls with it. We find comfort in it every time we face deep grief. Why is it so popular? Because it reminds us in profound ways how our Savior cares for us in the midst of our confusing lives. For this reason, Psalm 23 deserves a place in our study of salvation history.

---

*James Luther Mays, *Interpretation: Psalms* (Louisville: John Knox Press, 1994), 1.

CHAPTER **5**

Roller Coasters and the 23rd Psalm

by Dan Boone

ARE YOU A ROLLER-COASTER DAREDEVIL? If you are, you're familiar with Space Mountain, the Vortex, the Wabash Cannonball, or that old, unnamed, creaky, wooden roller coaster at the state fair.

My youngest daughter is making life difficult for me these days. Abby grew past the height restriction line that keeps little kids off fast roller coasters. The other day she walked up to the Wabash Cannonball, checked her height, and loudly announced, "Hey, Dad, let's ride this one together." What male adult wants to look chicken in the eyes of his adventurous child?

The first part of the ride is slow . . . tension-building slow . . . agonizing slow. I hear each clink of the giant chains and spokes as they pull us past the treetops, beyond Ferris-wheel height, somewhere near small-plane vicinity. Then, *whoosh!* As the machine plunges toward earth, I can taste my lunch—again. I am white-knuckling the safety bar. Abby has both hands in the air. Just about the time the roller-coaster plunge is bottoming out (and I am considering breathing), it jerks sharply into a right bank turn—then into a double upside-down loop—then a sudden left into the loading zone. The next sound I hear is air brakes. The safety bar lifts, and someone else is stepping into our seats.

As we walk away, Abby looks at me and asks, "Dad, which part did you like best?" Which part? How do you dissect a blur? You can't analyze a wild roller-coaster ride second by second. I suppose my favorite part was walking away alive.

The whole thing reminds me of life. It starts slowly and then speeds up. It has its peaks and plunges, plenty of sharp turns and unexpected loops that take your breath away. About the time you're ready to relax, your ride is over, and someone else is stepping into your place. In "roller coasterology" terms, life's a blur.

The Psalms and Life

Here's why I love the Psalms: they are a collection of frozen moments, snapshots, and arrested blurs. Psalms dissect blurs. As we read the Book of Psalms, we recognize that it captures life in one of three places: the pit, the rock, or the mountaintop.

The Pit. In the pit, life is hard. Evil is winning. There are enemies galore. The bad guys are getting all the good breaks. God seems absent. Life isn't fair. The writers of these pit psalms are frustrated, abandoned, vengeful, angry. They are not enjoying the ride, and they don't mind complaining to the establishment. They want it to stop now! They want their money back. One-third of the Psalms looks at life from the perspective of the pit.

The Rock. The rock is the solid ledge just outside the pit. You can still see the fingernail scratch marks around the lip of the pit. They got out. They finally made it! On the rock you find lots of emotion, exuberance, and excitement. Absence has turned to Presence. Weeping has turned to joy. Sackcloth has been traded for dancing shoes. On the rock you hear words like "hallelujah," "praise the LORD," and "amen." Roller-coaster riders fling their hands in the air and relish the wind in their face.

The Mountaintop. From the perspective of the mountaintop, we get a bird's-eye view of the whole of life. The anguish of the pit is gone but remembered. The exuberance of the rock has faded but is remembered. Depth replaces passion. Loud emotion gives way to quiet confidence.

Psalm 23 was written on the mountaintop. The psalmist looked back over the whole of life and remembered "the valley of the shadow of death" and the presence of enemies. He has ridden the ride. He has been there. He can tell you about pits and rocks in detail, but he doesn't. He leans back in his easy chair and reflects on the whole journey. He says,

> The LORD is my shepherd, I shall not be in want.
>   He makes me lie down in green pastures,
> he leads me beside quiet waters,
>   he restores my soul.
> He guides me in paths of righteousness
>   for his name's sake.
> Even though I walk
>   through the valley of the shadow of death,
> I will fear no evil,
>   for you are with me;
> your rod and your staff,
>   they comfort me.
>
> You prepare a table before me
>   in the presence of my enemies.
> You anoint my head with oil;
>   my cup overflows.
> Surely goodness and love will follow me
>   all the days of my life,
> and I will dwell in the house of the LORD
>   forever.

We hesitate to tinker with this psalm. Dealing with the

23rd psalm piecemeal does not enhance its wholeness and beauty. We don't need exegetical scalpels, but a shift occurs in the psalm that we sometimes miss. Images change suddenly without warning.

We begin as sheep. Sheep aren't shakers and movers. We don't control the destiny of nations. Wall Street doesn't rise and fall based on our bleating. We can't even keep ourselves alive without help. In this psalm we're chops and fleecy sweaters and Mary's pet who followed her to school one day. Where we live, water is scarce. Grass is rare. Heat is deadlier. We do not have it made in the shade.

Why then do we begin with "The LORD is my shepherd, I shall not be in want"? Either we're clueless sheep, or we have an awesome Shepherd. Apparently, the latter is the case. He beds us down in grassy meadows. He leads us to refreshing streams. He takes us along safe paths. He revives our life. He's a good Shepherd. He beats off beasts with His rod. He crook-necks us back onto the trail. He provides; we lack nothing. He protects; we fear no evil. He is with us. He's a good Shepherd. Sounds dreamy, doesn't it? It's a warm, cuddly psalm that ought to end "and they all lived happily ever after."

Some people check out on Christianity because of sentiment like this. They vehemently protest this superpositive, sugary, syrupy sweetness. They say, "Life's not that simple. I *do* want. I *do* have unmet needs. I *do* fear evil." They remind us that this is a world where factories shut down, stray bullets fly, taxes cut deeply, friends die too young, bigots exterminate races, truth masquerades, and homes come unglued. They say things like that—and they're right. If we listen carefully, we'll hear them say, "Forget grassy meadows and still waters and safe paths. This is here and now! Ain't no safe sheep in these parts." That's what they say as they check out on Christianity and decide to fend for themselves.

What do we have to say to that? Dare we validate the

reality of their perspective? Yes. Still, we also remind them of the perspective of this psalmist. He hasn't always lived on the mountaintop. He has been in the pit. He has done his share of lamenting in the pit. He has complained to the Shepherd. He didn't come to know this good Shepherd while grazing on Rebecca of Sunnybrook's farm. He didn't grow fat on the front lawn of Jed Clampett's mansion. He came to know this Shepherd in the valley where death's shadow lurked, where beasts stalked and killed, in a land where evil roamed unrestrained.

Our mountaintop conclusions about the shepherd are not spur-of-the-moment, tip-of-the-tongue, top-of-the-head passing thoughts. They are convictions gained across a lifetime. It takes a wise old sheep to write Psalm 23. When our generalizations about the Shepherd reach the ears of those still in the pits, we may sound too simplistic. The perspective of time is a necessary ingredient. If pit-dwellers persist, their exuberance on the mountaintop will someday be as real as their anguish in the pit.

Climbing the Mountain

Midway through the psalm there is a shift. We've been sheep. Now we remove our sheepskins and pile them neatly in the corner. We leave the safety of our air-conditioned comfort and walk outside into a 100-degree day. We start running down the street. Gangs with knives chase us. We dare not stop for shade or water. If they catch us, we're dead. We are now pursued, hounded travelers. We're running for our lives, and the nearest town is miles away. Our enemy is closing in on us. Our lips are cracked and bleeding. Our heads are beet red, burned by the sun. Our tongues are thick and dry. There are blisters on our feet. We're ready to collapse. If we do, we die. We can't go on— but we must. Our knees almost buckle as we struggle up the steep sand dune.

We top the mound, and there it is—an encampment in

the desert. We stumble into the camp. A Provider greets us and does unbelievable things. He puts cool, soothing lotion on our heads. He keeps our lemonade glass filled to the brim. He spreads a feast in the presence of our enemies, who scowl at us from the top of the last sand dune. He offers safe haven. What a wonderful surprise! Just when we thought we couldn't go on, this One appeared at the point of our need. He provides; we lack nothing. What a gracious Host!

Looking back over our lives, we realize the places where evil almost caught us. The places we almost fell to temptation, threw in the towel, behaved destructively, gave up. We remember persons who almost ruined our lives, bitterness that almost consumed us, tragedies that almost sabotaged our faith. Yet there in the desert we stumbled into the arms of a grace-filled One who treated us better than we could have imagined. He saved us from certain ruin. What a gracious Host!

It is no wonder that the psalm concludes, in effect, "Surely goodness and mercy have followed me all the days of my life. I want to live forever in the presence of my good Shepherd and my gracious Host."

Conclusion

I love to hear the words that tumble down from the mountain in cascading certainty. Granted, those words sound a little too simple for the shakers and movers who clock in and out of the dog-eat-dog world. And sometimes mountaintop music is out-decibeled by pit dirges and rock tunes. Yet the closer I get to the end of the ride, the more I like the music from the mountain.

Life's a blur. It starts slowly and speeds up. It has its peaks and plunges, plenty of sharp turns and unexpected loops that take your breath away. About the time you're ready to relax, your ride is over and someone else is stepping into your place. In "roller coasterology" terms, life's a blur. Listen to the mountain music. Believe what you hear. God is a good Shepherd. God is a gracious Host. He provides; we lack nothing. He protects; we fear nothing. Maybe Abby was right to have both hands in the air instead of white-knuckling the bar. Enjoy the ride!

About the author: Dan Boone, D.Min., is senior pastor of Kankakee College Church of the Nazarene, Bourbonnais, Illinois. In 1993 he was named Preacher of the Year by Nazarene Theological Seminary. He also serves as an adjunct professor at Olivet Nazarene University and is on the board of trustees at Nazarene Theological Seminary.

Psalm 51

INTRODUCTION

Psalm 51 ranks among the best-known psalms. While many of the other well-known ones are hymns of praise, Psalm 51 is the model for every penitent sinner.

David wrote this psalm after the prophet Nathan had confronted him about his sin with Bathsheba. (See 2 Samuel 12:1-15.) David's sin was despicable. He committed adultery and murder. Yet he learned from this experience that God's salvation extends to every repentant sinner, regardless of the sin committed. The depth of David's repentance recorded in the words of this psalm leaves us a pattern for our own repentance.

Some claim that parts of Psalm 51 have been repeated more often in worship and personal devotions than any other scripture. Given the power of sin to bring unparalleled destruction and despair, this claim is probably true.

Christians find many uses for the words of Psalm 51. "It has been used as a penitential prayer, as the proper psalm to introduce the season of Lent, as a hymn in metrical version, as a regular prayer of confession, as a source for liturgical sentences, and as a text for reflection on Christian doctrine."*

Psalm 51 deserves a place in our study of salvation history because of its penitential tone. Since God has written the law on our hearts, we are well aware if we break God's law. Yet God has not made us aware just to leave us in a state of misery. He provides a way of escape when we repent, and He shows us how to repent. We might have no better example than the words left us by a sorrowful King David.

---

*James Luther Mays, *Interpretation: Psalms* (Louisville: John Knox Press, 1994), 197-8.

CHAPTER 6

Returning to the Right Way

by John N. Oswalt

TODAY A FATHER DETERMINED that he would not slap his daughter when she "smart-mouthed" him. Yet when she cursed him, he not only slapped her but hit her with his fist.

How can he deal with that heavy, gnawing feeling inside that keeps telling him that he has failed, again? He will probably choose one of two ways popular today. One way is to *deny that what he did was wrong.* "She deserved it," he might say, "for acting that way." Or if he can't escape guilt by denying that what he did was wrong, he might try the other way—*deny that he is responsible* for what he has done. The father says, "Yes, knocking my daughter down like that was wrong of me, but really no one should blame me for it." Perhaps it happened because his parents abused him as a child. Or perhaps his boss recently fired him from a job. Or maybe his wife left him. Or maybe a medication had left him irritable and short-tempered. Whatever the excuse given, he is saying, "I am not responsible for my actions. I am a victim of circumstances beyond my control. Though I may have behaved in a wrong way, I am not really guilty."

Nevertheless, when we try to deny our guilt feelings by denying responsibility, at least two disastrous effects occur. The first is that denial drives guilt underground. We may deny the reality of our guilt on the surface of our minds, but our subconscious personality knows better. As a result, the subconscious attempts to find other ways to rid itself of the burden.

The second effect is that we fail to grow. As we exercise responsible choices, we develop character. Only when we accept responsibility for our choices—some good and some bad—can we learn how to live with the outcomes and to grow through them.

A Better Way

If neither denial of wrongdoing nor denial of responsibility is the right way for dealing with our guilt, what is? It is King David's way, as recorded for us in Psalm 51.

David was no sinless man. In fact, he sinned terribly, as reported in 2 Samuel 11—12. His first instinct was to try to cover up what he had done. Then he compounded his sin with an even worse sin, still trying to protect himself. Nevertheless, the good news is that God would not abandon David. He found a way to get David to face his responsibility. When David opened his eyes to see that, he could also see the way back to forgiveness, freedom, and health. In what David saw, we can find the way back too.

Above everything else, David saw what sin really is and does. We can never get back to the right way until we see with the same clarity. David saw that although sin reveals itself in outward acts, those acts spring from a set of attitudes and inner conditions that are the real problem.

David lamented this inner corruption in verses 5 and 6 and cried out to God for a radical change in those attitudes and conditions. He used three different words to describe sin in verses 2 and 3. The first is our word "sin." It connotes that tendency of ours to miss the targets of life. We draw the bow back, take careful aim, and then in despair watch the arrow curve away from the bull's-eye. Sometimes we miss the target intentionally, wanting something other than what we should. That's what David did. Instead of the faithfulness and self-denial God meant for us to achieve, David chose to aim for a few moments of stolen pleasure at no cost to himself. In fact, he missed that target too. All he got was agony, tragedy, and death.

Why is this? Why do we so consistently miss the targets of life, whether intentionally or unintentionally? It lies in the second word David used to describe his condition. It is the word "iniquity." Sometimes the Hebrew word here is translated "guilt." It speaks of the twistedness in us that both leads *to* sin and results *from* sin. David recognized that something in us prefers the tainted to the pure, the dark to the light, the prohibited to the permitted. Our arrows will not fly true because they are all subtly twisted. Nowhere is this condition more powerfully expressed than in Romans 7 where Paul, speaking as a good Jew, lamented the helplessness of *knowing* what is right to make us *do* what is right.

David used a third word, and it was perhaps the most meaningful of all for him. It is the word "transgression." Transgression speaks of rebellion, that intentional refusal to remain within prescribed bounds. It is that in us that says "I won't" instead of "I will." Often it is irrational. The thing commanded is actually something we would like to do, but just because someone commanded it, we will not do it.

David looked at his own behavior in this awful light. He was no chained, beaten slave of a terrible taskmaster. David had followed God gladly, and in return God had given him the highest place in the Kingdom. Yet David had turned and slapped his Master in the face. It is no wonder that what he had done horrified David himself.

Why was what David did to Bathsheba and Uriah wrong? Because it was an offense against God's holy law. Today we attempt to create ethical standards while denying that there are any standards written into the nature of the universe. We make a great deal of persons' "rights," trying to define the rightness or wrongness of an act on the basis of whether we infringed on anyone's liberties. However, this is very slippery ground. If rights are the only basis of ethics, then ultimately those with the power can justify almost any action. That is precisely what David had done. As king he had the right (or power) to take any woman in the kingdom and to consign any soldier to death. Still, with his painfully opened eyes, he now knew that it was not his or anyone else's rights that determine the rightness or wrongness of any action. He had broken the law of God and, as a result, had treated Bathsheba and Uriah—indeed, his whole kingdom—in terribly wrong ways.

It's Time for a Change

If we are to return to the right way, as David did, it is time for us to stop covering up our sin, explaining it away, excusing it. Rather we must name it for what it is, recognizing its deep inner root and admitting that our behavior is wrong because it is an offense against the very nature of the universe as God made it.

David saw, and admitted, the effects of his sin upon his life. Above everything else, this psalm speaks of the defiling effects of sin. Three different times (in verses 2, 7, and 10) David asked God to make him clean again, to restore him to a condition of purity.

David recognized that his sins had robbed him of the peace he had once known. So he asked in verse 10 for a "steadfast," or a fixed, spirit. Earlier in life, the raging winds of life had threatened to drive his ship onto the rocks, but David had thrown out the anchors. They were hooked to an unshakable Rock, and the cables were firm. Yet, incredibly, David himself had taken an axe and cut the cables! His ship was again adrift, tossed this way and that.

David recognized that sin had destroyed the power of his testimony (vv. 12-15). Once he had seized every opportunity to tell the story of what God had done in his life. It may have first been done in stumbling and halting words, but those words had a power that seemed to strike hearers to the quick. Now he could tell that same story in much better words, smooth and eloquent ones. Yet it seemed as if they went about six inches out from his mouth and dropped to the ground like lead. They had no conviction or power about them. David had a hard time even getting his mouth open. Something had died, and David knew it. He had tried to ignore the fact or rationalize it during the previous year, but now he could only admit it and beg for God to open his mouth again (v. 15). He realized that God alone can break the guilt that has chained him. God alone once again can give him a "willing," or a volunteering, spirit (v. 12).

As terrible as all these effects of sin are, which David recognized, one more must have been the worst of all for him. It was the loss of the presence of God (v. 11).

Surely the memory of King Saul must have been written in letters of fire on David's mind at that time. David had seen Saul in those glorious days when God's Spirit had dramatically filled Saul and wonderfully used him. Yet he had also seen Saul when the Spirit of God was gone from him and another spirit altogether had come to fill the vacuum. How could he forget Saul's tragic end—dejected and rejected, frantically looking for light in the growing darkness? We can hear David cry out, "Oh no, not me too!"

However, David and Saul differed at this point. When Saul came face-to-face with the possible effects of his continued failure to obey God, his chief concern was with losing face before his people. So he begged Samuel, "Please honor me before the elders of my people and before Israel; come back with me, so that I may worship the LORD *your* God" (1 Samuel 15:30, emphasis added). However, David was not concerned about losing face; he was concerned about losing God! That is the cry of this psalm. God may take the kingdom, David's good name, and whatever else, but let Him not take His Holy Spirit. Let Him not take the blessed sense of His presence. David knew he could live without all those other things, but he could not live without God. Oh, how desperately we need to see the issue with the clarity David saw it: *the choice is sin or God,* and it can never be both.

Back to Square One

When we see the effects of our sin for what they really are, when we see the terrible price that sin must finally exact, then—and only then—hope exists that we may find our way back to the right way—God's way.

How do we get home? How do we get back to the right way? As important as it is to admit the nature of what we have done and to recognize the insidious nature that is at work in us, that doesn't get us home. As important as it is to admit what sin has cost and is costing us, that admission by itself does not get us back on the right way. What does? It is the third thing that David saw: the *cure* for sin. That cure lies in the nature and the acts of God. It is because of who He is and what He has done that it is possible for David and for us to be at home with God, our true home, again.

What is God's nature upon which David hurled himself? David's words in verse 11 of Psalm 51 reveal it. Notice what he said. *Not* "Give back your Holy Spirit." *Not* "Allow me back into your presence." Not "give back," but "do not . . . take." What does this mean? It means that in all those long months when David was denying the reality of what he had done and of what was happening to him, the Holy Spirit had not completely left him alone. He had kept on loving David, wooing him, drawing him. God is not a touchy lover, looking for the slightest chance to break up with us. No, His patience and mercy are almost limitless. To be sure, if David, seeing in unmistakable colors exactly what he had done and become, had refused to renounce all that, the Holy Spirit would have had no option but to depart. That is what had terrified David so. Yet until that moment, God would not let go of His child.

This was David's hope and ours: the patient and merciful character of God. It is not the quantity of our grief, nor the largeness of our promises to do better, nor the amount of our promised repayments that make forgiveness and restoration possible. Each of these may be desirable and necessary in given circumstances, but in the end only one thing can bring us home—the limitless love of God.

Yet the cure for sin lies not only in the *nature* of God but also in the *acts* of God. Though these actions are not directly stated, when we read the psalm in the light of all of God's revelation, we can see that it truly implies His actions here. How could God "blot out" the record of our transgressions (v. 1)? It was by means of the death of His Son Jesus Christ, hanging between His heaven and His earth, bleeding out His life to blot out the past with its sin. God's love cannot erase God's justice. The person who has sinned must die, just as the person who jumps from a tall building must strike the ground with killing force. Yet if God's Son himself were to die, then God's love could satisfy His justice, all supposing that the criminal will accept the offered pardon. Yes, God has blotted out our transgressions.

Getting It Right

What about the twisted self-absorption that makes the arrow always miss its true mark? What about the determined self-exaltation that makes every command to obey a hateful and detestable thing? Can we be cleansed from our iniquities? This was the age-long question of the Hebrew people. They had come to understand that the human spirit had a defect, one that prevented them from doing what they knew was right. Could the Spirit who had inhabited Moses, Gideon, David, and Isaiah also take up residence in them, falling over them like a gentle but irresistible rain to cleanse and renew? Of course, this is the very thing God planned to do (see Isaiah 32:15-16; Ezekiel 36:24-29). With the death of His Son to atone for the sins that prevented the Holy Spirit's residence, that residence became possible, not just for the few but for all. So David envisioned the kind of thorough washing that goes right down into the warp and woof of the cloth. No casual rinsing in a pail of tepid water for him! What he longed for could only be accomplished by the Holy Spirit in the washing of regeneration and the floodtide of sanctification.

What does it take to experience this merciful nature and these forgiving, cleansing acts? It is not religious behavior (v. 16). God doesn't want our religious behavior; He wants *us*. To be sure, when our hearts are right and our spirits are restored, religious activities are a very important way of showing what has happened to us. We are embodied spirits; the physical and the spiritual must always be held together. So, if I am sloppy and haphazard in my performance of religious activities, there is good reason to look sharply at the state of my soul. However, the activities are only an expression of the reality; they can never substitute for the reality itself. To try to use them in that way is pointless for us and disgusting for God (see Isaiah 1:10-15).

If we are to experience the love and forgiveness of God, "a broken spirit [and] a . . . contrite [crushed] heart" (v. 17) are required. Why should this be so? What sort of a monster-god delights in seeing us smashed? The physician who breaks a wrongly knit bone in order to set it right is no monster. Nor would it be an act of compassion to allow that grotesque joining to continue unmended. The sin problem is one of a failure-prone, twisted, rebellious spirit. Until we recognize that fact and are broken by it, there is little God can do for us. Until we hate sin in ourselves and are broken by its persistence, God's curing love is rendered ineffective. That's why it is so hard for "good" people to find God. They think that sin is merely bad actions and fail to see that sin is first of all a spiritual attitude. They are not broken by their pride and their self-righteousness, and so cannot fall at the feet of God, agreeing with Him about their true condition. Only when pride is squarely faced and surrendered to God may lasting victory over sin be experienced. Only when the spirit of pride is broken can we know in fullness an established, stable spirit; a free, willing spirit; and best of all, the Holy Spirit. Only then can we return to the right way.

About the author: John N. Oswalt, Ph.D., is professor of biblical studies at Asbury Theological Seminary in Wilmore, Kentucky.

Isaiah 53

INTRODUCTION

Isaiah was the name of a prophet in Israel whose career spanned the years from approximately 740 to 687 B.C. A book of the Bible bears his name. However, the debate about its authorship has raised the question: How many "Isaiahs" actually wrote the book?

The materials in the first 39 chapters are quite different from those of chapters 40 through 66. Some scholars have said this points to at least two different writers: the original Isaiah wrote a predictive message before the exile, and the second Isaiah recorded events after the Babylonian captivity. The traditional belief is that only one prophet and writer named Isaiah composed the book. He wrote all of the material as predictions. "Once prediction is regarded as a fundamental part of the prophet's message, there is no compelling reason for denying the unity of the book."*

When Isaiah wrote, Israel was in a precarious position because of the pressure from Assyria. That crisis resulted in the destruction of northern Israel and threatened the existence of southern Israel, namely Judah. The prophet's message was that only God would save the people and then only if they did not abandon Him. The Hebrew meaning of Isaiah's name pointed to the truth of the prophet's message. "Isaiah" means "Yahweh is salvation."

The 53rd chapter falls within the fourth and last of the "servant songs" of Isaiah. It is an important chapter for Christians. The New Testament applies this passage to Jesus on 10 occasions. Christian theology recognizes the messianic descriptions of the text and applies them to Jesus.

This is an important passage for us. In it we see a clear vision of the sufferings that would befall Christ on Calvary. This is the last Old Testament text of our study of salvation history, and it points directly to the coming Messiah.

*Harper Study Bible, ed. Harold Lindsell (Grand Rapids, Mich.: Zondervan Bible Publishers, 1965), 996.

CHAPTER 7

The Messiah Is Coming!

by Wayne McCown

THE MESSIAH IS COMING! Does your mind tingle at the thought? The excitement kindled should be like the feeling of a five-year-old being told, "Christmas is coming!"

Do you remember how, as a young child, you responded to the coming of Christmas—even months before the actual arrival of the big day?

Probably, your childish expectations were unrealistic and superficial. Santa did not come down the chimney as expected. You found no big bag filled with wished-for goodies. Nevertheless, Christmas still came. With its coming, there were choirs—not of angels, but of teenagers from your local church. There was a Christmas pageant—not with real shepherds, but with little boys in men's bathrobes. There also was a big holiday feast with special cookies—not brought by elves, but baked by Mom in the kitchen oven.

While the day may not have completely fulfilled your childish expectations, in reality it was better. In the essence of the Christmas celebration, there was a depth, a richness, a meaning that far surpassed your earlier excitement over pretty trees, bright lights, and big packages.

So it was with the coming of the Messiah. In the century preceding Jesus' birth, the religious culture of the Jews was rife with varied expectations of a coming Messiah.

Many expected Him to come as a conquering king who would deliver them from Roman rule. Many hoped His coming would introduce an era of prosperity and peace. Many thought He would establish a Jewish kingdom that would rule the earth.

His coming—the coming of Jesus Christ—did not quite match these expectations. Yet the reality of His coming was something far deeper, more meaningful, and longer lasting than these hopes and dreams.

Not that the deeper meaning of His coming had not been foreseen. It had been—by the prophets of the Old Testament. Particularly significant is the prophecy of Isaiah 53.

Of all the texts in the Old Testament, the New Testament writers more extensively quote Isaiah 53 than any other. If we were to lose the Old Testament altogether, we could reproduce most of Isaiah 53 from the New Testament. The New Testament authors extensively quote it in describing Jesus as our Savior. This shows its importance.

Isaiah 53 portrayed the coming Messiah, not as a conquering king, but as a Suffering Servant.

Our Human Need

Why would God send a *servant* to redeem us? Because of our human need.

Our Redeemer, as portrayed in this text, is one made like us in every respect. He knows "our infirmities" and "our sorrows" (v. 4). He bears "our transgressions" and "our iniquities" (v. 5).

Obviously, we need a Savior. However, God did not send one who is not able to sympathize with our weaknesses. Rather, He sent One who was tempted in every respect as we, "yet was without sin" (Hebrews 4:15).

Our deepest human problem is sin. Isaiah 53 acknowledged this fact, referring to our "transgressions," "iniquities," and "sin" no less than six times (in vv. 5, 6, 8, 11, 12).

I know a person—perhaps you do too—who has many personal problems. His physical ailments (which may be psychosomatic) have prevented him from working for more than a decade. His wife works to provide their support, and he whiles away his time. He also has serious emotional problems, bordering on the psychotic at times. Perhaps as a consequence, his relationships have suffered. His first marriage ended on the rocks some years ago. The children, now adolescents, have turned out weird and brought tremendous strain on the second marriage.

John* has a volatile temper and a vulgar mouth, which may reveal the source of his problems. His inner life is not in order. It sounds—and maybe looks—like a cesspool.

John's deepest need is not for more medication, counseling, or money—but cleansing.

Isaiah declared that the Messiah was coming to deal with our sin problem. That is good news!

A Man of Sorrows

The Messiah meets our deepest need, the prophet declared, by coming in the form of a servant. Isaiah 53 portrayed Him, though anointed of God, as a Suffering Servant. Isaiah used strong, graphic terms to depict His suffering: "a man of sorrows, and acquainted with grief" (v. 3, KJV); "pierced . . . crushed" (v. 5); "oppressed and afflicted" (v. 7).

Most surprising is the declaration that God has a role in all of this. "[He was] stricken by God, smitten by him, and afflicted" (v. 4). "It was the LORD's will to crush him and cause him to suffer" (v. 10). The Messiah's suffering would fulfill God's plan of redemption.

Personally, we find it hard to accept suffering and to understand how it can serve God's purpose.

The prophet Jeremiah was a person who suffered terribly, especially in fulfilling the divine commission in his life. Frequently, he complained to God about his trials and tribulations. They were more emotional and social than physical but very real nonetheless. He felt unappreciated, ostracized, and generally put upon. (Have you ever been there?)

"Why, O Lord?" he cried in many ways. (We know Jeremiah as "the weeping prophet.") Not only was the suffering itself painful but so was his struggle to understand God's purpose in it all.

Poured Out for Us

Like Jeremiah, the Messiah would be a "man of sorrows." Nevertheless, you ask, how could His suffering redeem *us?* The short answer is this: because He suffered for us, in our place, taking our sin and punishment upon himself to save us.

The life and mission of the Suffering Servant ended in a violent death. "He was led like a lamb to the slaughter" (v. 7). "By oppression and judgment he was taken away" (v. 8). "He was assigned a grave with the wicked" (v. 9).

More than a tragic ending to another human life, this man's death was an offering for sin. Isaiah 53 says, "He poured out his life unto death. . . . For he bore the sin of many" (v. 12). He took our sin upon himself; "the punishment that brought us peace was upon him" (v. 5). As a part of the divine plan of redemption, "the LORD makes his life a guilt offering" (v. 10).

All of us have observed instances where one person's suffering benefited another. Often, parents suffer for the benefit of their children. It may be as small as foregoing a pleasure so their children may enjoy one.

Other sacrifices are more prolonged and burdensome. I have observed families make tremendous sacrifices over many years so their children might have the benefit of a Christian-college education.

I have also seen parents support their children through difficult crises, even though that support entailed great anguish and pain for them. I know personally the suffering parents sometimes bear. When my younger son—an exceptionally bright and gifted young man— turned to alcohol during his teen years, I felt he had put a dagger through my heart. I wept for days. Though terribly hurt, disappointed, and distraught, I continued to love and support him—until, by God's grace, he regained his senses (and his salvation!).

Isaiah said the Suffering Servant died for *us*, in *our* stead, that *we* might be forgiven of our sins, personally reconciled to God, healed, and made whole. His blood saves us.

Christ Suffered for You

These prophecies of the Old Testament find their New Testament fulfillment in Jesus. Especially noteworthy for its Christian application of Isaiah 53 is 1 Peter 2:18-25.

Here the apostle portrayed Jesus as God's servant who in His suffering fulfilled—quite specifically—the prophecies of Isaiah 53. Quoting from Isaiah, Peter told us about Jesus: "'He committed no sin, and no deceit was found in his mouth.' When they hurled their insults at him, he did not retaliate; . . . he made no threats. . . . by his wounds you have been healed" (vv. 22-24). These descriptions are all direct quotations from Isaiah 53, applied personally to Jesus. Clearly, Peter regarded Him as the fulfillment of the Suffering Servant prophesied by Isaiah.

Jesus is the Messiah! Nevertheless, how did He come down to us? Not as a conquering king but as a servant.

According to the Epistle to the Hebrews, God's Son humbled himself and became one with us. Because His concern was for humankind, He came as a human being. "For this reason he had to be made like his brothers in every way, in order that he might become a merciful and faithful high priest in service to God, and that he might make atonement for the sins of the people" (2:17).

As a human, Jesus suffered our temptations, pain, and sorrow. "Because he . . . suffered when he was tempted, he is able to help those who are being tempted" (v. 18). "For we do not have a high priest who is unable to sympathize with our weaknesses, but we have one who has been tempted in every way, just as we are—yet was without sin" (4:15).

Moreover, in Jesus' identification with our human condition, we find a source of strong encouragement: "Let us then approach the throne of grace with confidence, so that we may receive mercy and find grace to help us in our time of need" (4:16).

In His Steps

As God's servant, Jesus suffered in obedience to the Father's will *for you and me.*

His purpose was to lead us back to God, "For you were like sheep going astray" (1 Peter 2:25). "He himself bore our sins in his body on the tree, so that we might die to sins and live for righteousness" (v. 24).

Moreover, in His suffering for us, Christ left us an example of how to live. Jesus calls us, as His followers, to imitate His conduct in the face of adversity, abuse, and death. "When they hurled their insults at him, he did not retaliate; when he suffered, he made no threats. Instead, he entrusted himself to [God] who judges justly" (v. 23).

During my time as a senior administrative executive at a Christian college, Sharon served as my secretary and administrative assistant. A godly woman with a big heart, she ministered God's grace and love to all those around her. As part of an annual mammogram, they discovered a suspicious lump in her breast. Surgery confirmed the doctor's suspicions—the lump was malignant. They removed as many of the lymph nodes as possible. Twenty-three of the nodes proved to be cancerous, signaling the spread of cancer in her body. They prescribed aggressive chemotherapy, followed by radiation treatments.

None of us would wish this on a friend, let alone a family member. Yet we all know someone—probably a Christian brother or sister—who has had to undergo this same kind of experience. Moreover, it could happen to any of us: Cancer—like death—is no respecter of persons.

The real question is this: How do we respond when tested? Do we rail against God, asking, "Why me?" Do we become disillusioned and lose faith in God's love, purpose, and provision for us? Do we fall prey to temptation? Or do we witness to God's presence with us in the midst of the furnace?

Sharon's response proved her mettle to all those around her. In the midst of her trials—which were many— she continued to give a clear witness to the Lord's sanctifying presence in her life. I have before me an E-mail message she posted at the college, about one month into her ordeal. Although Sharon did not intend it for public reading, she has given me permission to share it with you. I do so with no editing at all. It is a private window into the grace of God currently at work in the life of Sharon and our college community.

My chemo was canceled this week due to very low blood counts. My surgery has been scheduled for Monday to have the mediport inserted. This will give the nurses a much easier access for administering chemo and for drawing blood, since they can only use my left arm for such purposes, the right arm is off limits because of my previous surgery. I will then have chemo on Tuesday and Wednesday afternoons.

The Lord's timing is perfect, and He is in control. God knew what was best concerning the timing for the mediport. "The LORD is good, a strong hold in the day of trouble; and he knoweth them that trust in him" (Nahum 1:7, KJV). "Through God we shall do valiantly: for he it is that shall tread down our enemies" (Psalm 108:13, KJV). God holds each one of us in the palm of His hand. God knows best what cross we need to bear and His grace is sufficient.

Thank you again for your faithful prayers and continued words of encouragement. May the Lord draw you close to Him each time you enter your prayer closet!

We are called to "follow in his steps" (1 Peter 2:21). He is our "Shepherd" (v. 25) and has left for us "an example"

(v. 21). The Greek terms here are very colorful, suggesting that Jesus' behavior is a *pattern* that we are to carefully *trace.* We, too, are to be servants—of God and one another—willing to suffer for righteousness' sake. Thus, may we fulfill our calling, by following Christ.

Jesus, Our Messiah

Jesus is our Messiah! Though God's Son and the Anointed One, He came down to us as the Suffering Servant. During His days on earth, He suffered—on *our* behalf, in *our* stead, for *our* sins. Through sorrow, suffering, and death, He secured our redemption. His blood saves us.

He also left us an example, as to how we ought to live. When the going gets rough, we may look to Him. In the midst of pain and persecution, He retained His trust in God the Father, and a right attitude toward those around Him. "Father, forgive them," He cried, "for they do not know what they are doing" (Luke 23:34).

Although the nails still hurt—and so did the rejection—Jesus did not spew forth curses. Instead, even as He hung on the Cross, He ministered God's grace to the dying thief and to His forlorn mother. This is the example we are called to imitate, to trace, in our daily lives.

Jesus is our Example. He has come to save us from our sins and to show us how to live in righteousness before God. He also is our coming Messiah who will return to earth someday and take us to heaven to live with Him. Oh, what a day that will be! Are you looking forward to it? Are you ready to meet Him, our coming King?

---

*Name has been changed.

About the author: Wayne McCown, Ph.D., is senior vice president for academic affairs and provost, as well as professor of biblical studies, at Roberts Wesleyan College in Rochester, New York.

John 1

INTRODUCTION

With the Gospel of John we turn a new page in the story of salvation. We enter the world of the New Testament with its fulfillments of Old Testament prophecies. We see the characteristics of God take on human form in the Person of Jesus.

The majestic beginning words of Genesis echo in our ears as we hear the breathtaking opening of John: "In the beginning was the Word, and the Word was with God, and the Word was God" (1:1). That verse starts an 18-verse prologue whose profound ideas and eloquent words sound more like a musical symphony than literature.

The words and images of the Gospel of John have become favorites of millions of Christians down through the centuries. As one writer said it clearly: "John . . . has the most penetrating gaze into the eternal mysteries and the eternal truths, and into the very mind of God. It is true that there are many people who find themselves closer to God and to Jesus Christ in *John* than in any other book in the world."[1]

John's Gospel, sometimes called the Gospel of Love, is often recommended to new Christians as the part of the Bible to read first. Yet after multiple readings, the book still holds rich beauty for all Christians. One writer described it as "a pool in which a child may wade and an elephant can swim. It is both simple and profound."[2]

The Gospel writer clearly stated the purpose of the book in chapter 20: "These are written that you may believe that Jesus is the Christ, the Son of God, and that by believing you may have life in his name" (v. 31). Any discussions about the origins of this book are of little consequence when compared to the importance of what was written. The words of John's Gospel are about "the Word," the divine Logos. John introduces us to an eternally existent Word who took on the flesh of humanity and lived among us. This is the chapter of salvation history that made it possible for humans to come face-to-face with our Creator.

---

1. William Barclay, *The Gospel of John* (Philadelphia: The Westminster Press, 1955), xv.

2. Leon Morris, *The Gospel According to John* (Grand Rapids, Mich.: Wm. B. Eerdmans Publishing Co., 1971), 7.

CHAPTER 8

The Word We Could Touch

by Carol J. Rotz

THE PREACHER WAS SPEAKING loudly, trying to project his voice so that his audience of senior citizens could hear his message. The poor acoustics of the retirement home's dining hall did not help. The young pastor was speaking words of love from the greatest love story ever. He could hear a softly voiced "amen" from time to time. However, from the other side of the potted plants, in the far corner of the room, came an angry response. At the repeated use of "Jesus," a woman indignantly called out, "Watch your tongue, Sonny!" She was trying to protect the name of her Lord. She did not hear the words about the Word of God. She thought the young man, like so many others, was using the Lord's name blasphemously.

Outside of church, the word *Jesus* is just a word. The precious name of Jesus is often used casually by people who don't know the Living Word. For too many people, the Bible with its message of love and life is a closed book. Yet the question of who Jesus is, as well as our response to Him, is central. It is the most important question anyone will ever have to face. We all have to answer it eventually—in this world or in the one to come. It is important because the quality of our lives—now and forever—depends on our answer to the question, "Who is Jesus?"

John's Story of Jesus

John told us that he wrote his Gospel to help people find an answer. He wanted them to know and love Jesus. "These are written that you may believe that Jesus is the Christ, the Son of God, and that by believing you may have life in his name" (20:31). John was probably addressing those who did not yet believe that Jesus was God. He wrote to challenge them to a decision of faith. It may be, though, that he wrote to those who already believed. He may have written to strengthen their faith, to help them to continue to believe. The purpose would then read: "These are written that you *may maintain your belief* that Jesus is the Christ."

Certainly John's Gospel speaks today to those of us who are believers. Through it we can learn more about who Jesus is. It challenges us to respond with greater faith. It also provides the basis for faith for those who do not know who He is. Yet the Gospel is not a theological treatise. It has a lot of wonderful theology in it, but John did not set out a list of dogmatic statements to memorize. He told a story that challenges us to respond.

The Beginning of the Story

This story actually began in the first chapter of Genesis. John returned to this beginning and brought the story to its climax in the Person of Jesus Christ. Just as Genesis 1 sets the foundation and context for the rest of the Bible, so the first chapter of John introduces the Gospel. The first verse tells us that in the beginning the Word was with God and actually was God. The Jews understood "the word of God" to be the self-assertion of the divine personality. For the Greeks it denoted the rational mind that ruled the universe. John spoke to both the Jewish people and the Gentile world when he proclaimed that the Word is Jesus. Jesus is eternal. He has always existed. John did not try to prove this assertion. He did not try to verify Jesus' deity or His humanity. He simply told the story of Jesus' life, death, and resurrection.

The Prologue

John's introductory chapter divides quite naturally into two parts. The first 18 verses give a retrospective overview of the Gospel. John summarized Jesus' mission from a post-Easter perspective. He shared from firsthand experience (v. 14), and he introduced another witness also named John. The Gospel writer told of John the Baptist, who told of Jesus, who revealed God.

Bible scholars often call the first eighteen verses the prologue because they summarize the Gospel story. The prologue invites the reader into the story. These beautiful verses provide the background of Jesus' existence before time (v. 1) and the wonder of His incarnation—His becoming one of us (v. 14). In this passage we see the plan of salvation. God sent Jesus to be the light of the world (vv. 3-5); to bring grace, truth (v. 17), and blessings (v. 16); to reveal God (v. 18); and to provide salvation (vv. 12-13). Unfortunately, many did not receive this Creator-Savior (vv. 10-11), but those who did became children of God (vv. 12-13).

Jesus Came to the World

So John's story begins with an overview of Jesus' person and His work, of the tragedy of His rejection, and of the glory of His presence. Jesus is the focus of the entire Gospel, and this first chapter introduces Him to us. John omitted the birth narratives included in Matthew and Luke. He moved from the summary of Jesus' preexistence, mission, and rejection to the calling of the first disciples. John's description of Jesus is rich with words full of meaning. Here is John's answer to the question, "Who is Jesus?"

Jesus is the Logos, the Word, who was with God in the beginning and who was God (v. 1). He is the Creator. Through Him the world and all things were made (vv. 3,

10). In Him is life (v. 4), and He is the light (v. 7), "the true light that gives light to every [human]" (v. 9). He became flesh and "camped" among us (v. 14). He is God's only Son (vv. 14, 18, 34, 49), was sent by God (v. 14), and is at God's side (v. 18). He makes the Father known (v. 18). He is "the Son of Man" (v. 51), "the Lord" (v. 23), "Rabbi" or "Teacher" (v. 38), "the Messiah" or "Christ" (Anointed One) (v. 41). He is the "Lamb of God" (vv. 29, 36) who takes away the sin of the world. His name is Jesus (vv. 36-38, 42-50), "the son of Joseph" (v. 45). He comes after John the Baptist and has "surpassed" him (vv. 15, 27, 30). Jesus is "full of grace and truth" (vv. 14, 17), and through His grace "we have all received one blessing after another" (v. 16). The Spirit came down from heaven as a dove and remained on Jesus (v. 33), and He "will baptize with the Holy Spirit" (v. 33). Heaven will open, and the angels of God will ascend and descend on Jesus (v. 51).

Jesus Came for Everyone

Wonder and adoration can be the only response to the Jesus presented in John 1. The emphasis is not, however, on a God who is far away, waiting to receive worship. Remember that the purpose of the Gospel is to help people believe in Jesus and have life in Him (20:31). Remember that Jesus came so that those who believe might become children of God. John included people in this first chapter who represent all those for whom Jesus came. We are challenged to identify with them. John portrayed those who responded to Jesus as examples of faith or of unbelief.

The simple, wonderful truth is that Jesus came for all people (1:7). John personalizes this with the pronouns "us," "we," and "all" (vv. 14,16). These words include everyone. Personalize those verses for yourself: "Jesus is *my* light. Through Him *I* can believe. If *I* believe Him, if *I* receive Him and believe in His name, He gives *me* the right to become a child of God. *I* have received one blessing after another through the fullness of His grace." John summarized this wonderful universality again in chapter 3, verse 16: "For God so loved the world that he gave his one and only Son, that *whoever* [that is, *everyone*] believes in him shall not perish but have eternal life" (emphasis added).

Some Were Seekers

The inclusiveness is one of opportunity. Jesus came for everyone, but He does not force himself on anyone. Some seek but make no decision. In this first chapter of John, the Jews in Jerusalem sent priests, Levites (v. 19), and Pharisees (v. 24) to question John the Baptist. The Jews discovered that John the Baptist was not the Christ (v. 20). However, nothing indicates that they sought out Jesus, who was standing among them. The Jews were looking for the Christ, the Anointed One promised in their Scriptures. These who studied the Scriptures should have been the first to recognize Him, to answer the question, "Who is Jesus?"

Some Were Rejecters

In this passage John did not tell us of the Jew's rejection of Jesus. Their opposition to Jesus becomes clear later in the Gospel. At this point they merely fail to follow up in their quest for the Messiah. Of course, a "no decision" is the same as rejection. Tragically, there are those who make a conscious decision of rejection. John calls them "the darkness" (v. 5), which did not understand or overcome the light. They are "the world" (v. 10). They are Jesus' "own" (v. 11). The Jews were looking for Him under the guidance of their Scriptures, but they did not recognize Him. And Paul contended in Romans 1:18-20 and 3:9, both Jews *and* Gentiles have had ample opportunity to know their Lord. How unfortunate that so many whom He has created fail to recognize Him as their Lord.

Some Were Accepters

Fortunately, there are those who accept and receive life. John assured us that all who receive Jesus, who believe on His name, are "born of God" (v. 12). Jesus came for everyone. Some inquire but do not come close enough to make a decision. Others reject. Some believe and receive life. In this first chapter of John, five became Jesus' disciples. In an important way the opening of the Gospel is as much about the origins of the believers as it is about the origins of Jesus. The first 12 chapters of John tell of the many persons and events that testify to who Jesus is.

One of the key words of John 1—and the whole Gospel—is "testimony." John the Baptist is the key witness (vv. 7, 8, 34). He was a man whom God sent "to testify concerning [the] light, so that . . . all men might believe" (vv. 6, 7). He baptized with water to reveal Jesus to Israel (v. 31). He was not the Christ (vv. 20, 25), Elijah (vv. 21, 25), or "the Prophet" (vv. 22, 25). He was an eyewitness, and as such he testified that Jesus was "the Son of God" (v. 34). He equated himself with the Old Testament prophet Isaiah as "the voice of one calling in the desert, 'Make straight the way for the Lord'" (v. 23, quoting Isaiah 40:3).

John the Baptist was an influential man who attracted the attention of the Jews in Jerusalem. He had disciples. He could have protected himself and his reputation. He could have built his following. Instead, he told them of Jesus. He introduced his followers to the Messiah. His job was to pave the way. The prologue provides an overview of John the Baptist's witnessing ministry and testimony. In verse 19 the action begins. John the Baptist pointed his disciples to Jesus. In succeeding scenes, these new believers also became witnesses.

Some Were Witnesses

In the first scene (vv. 19-28) John was baptizing at Bethany (on the east side of the Jordan River) when some priests and Levites came to question him. John gave his testimony, clearly pointing them to Christ.

The next day John the Baptist saw Jesus and gave his testimony (vv. 29-34). He proclaimed that Jesus was the Son of God, "the Lamb of God, who takes away the sin of the world!" (v. 29). John the Baptist confirmed his testimony with an account of the Spirit coming down from heaven like a dove (vv. 32-34).

In the next scene (vv. 35-42) two of John the Baptist's disciples followed Jesus. First, John the Baptist pointed Jesus out as the Lamb of God. Then they talked to Jesus himself and followed Him. One of those disciples was Andrew. The first thing he did was to find his brother Simon Peter and bring him to Christ.

Scene four (vv. 43-51) took place the next day. This time, Jesus found Philip. Philip then found Nathanael, witnessed to him, and brought him to Jesus. Nathanael was doubtful at first but fully believed when Jesus spoke to him.

What a chain of events! In just four days five people came to believe in Jesus and follow Him. John the Baptist pointed his disciples to Jesus. One of those disciples found his brother Simon (Peter) and brought him to Jesus. Jesus found Philip, and Philip found Nathanael and brought him to Jesus. The converts became missionaries to others.

Telling the Story

Here is a model for network evangelism—people finding Jesus and helping others to find Him. The pattern as recorded in John 1:35-50 is simple:

- The believer finds and evangelizes someone else.
- The believer identifies Jesus.
- The believer leads the person to Jesus.
- Jesus sees the newcomer and speaks a confirming word.

What could be simpler? The most important question anyone will ever face is, "Who is Jesus?" Once we recognize Him and believe in Him, we become the children of God. And that is just the beginning. We then have the privilege of introducing others to our Lord. We become witnesses, and the task is surprisingly simple. Find people and let them know that you have found Jesus. Tell them who Jesus is, then take them to Him. Jesus will know how best to speak to them. The best witness is Jesus' own person, the words that He speaks, and the things He does.

"If only it were that simple," you say. "Peter made a wonderful, colorful disciple, but you don't know *my* brother. If *I* were to go to my friend having a picnic under a tree . . ." The point is, Jesus saw Nathanael under the fig tree before Philip called him. Jesus knew you before anyone brought you to Him, and He is already with that unlikely brother or friend. Our task is not to convince them. Our task is not to fill them with doctrinal arguments or pious phrases. We are simply to *introduce* them to Jesus, who was with God from the beginning and who is himself God.

The Gospel of John tells the story of the Word of God who became human to reveal God. Proclaiming doctrinal positions is easier than professing the faith the fourth Gospel demands. John records a struggle between those who acknowledge Jesus as the revealer of God and those who will not. This struggle will go on until the end of the story. Jesus remains the same. He is the Light, even though the darkness does not understand it. But the darkness cannot overcome it. Just as darkness is a sharp contrast to light, so rejection is a direct opposite of reception. Our privilege and responsibility remain the same. Our task is to tell the wonderful story of Jesus through our words and through our actions. We must tell the story clearly so that everyone can hear and respond.

About the author: Rev. Carol J. Rotz is deputy vice chancellor for academics at Africa Nazarene University. She is also a candidate for the Litt.D. in philosophy at Rand Afrikaans University.

Matthew 5:3-12, 17-20

INTRODUCTION

Matthew, one of the prominent disciples and one whom the Master had called away from a tax collector's booth, had a deep concern for the Jews nearly a generation after Jesus' death and resurrection. He wanted to prove to them that Jesus of Nazareth was their Messiah. However, he had a bit of a problem.

It appears that Mark's written account had been circulating for several years. Mark's Gospel gave the narrative of Jesus' life and actions in a bare-bones way. Mark used very few words to describe the entire earthly journey of Jesus. Matthew wanted to make sure the Jews understood the Jewishness of Jesus. He did this primarily by using much of Mark's material and showing how Jesus' life and ministry fulfilled the Old Testament Scriptures.

Why would an eyewitness like Matthew depend heavily on Mark's account? The answer seems to be that he agreed with the accuracy of Mark's testimony about Jesus but wanted to more fully address the Messiah issue for the Jews.

The focus of our study in this chapter is what we often call the Sermon on the Mount. Here we find the Master unfolding practical ways that enable us to live Christlike lives. The Sermon on the Mount contains most of the theological teachings of Jesus. In them, He moves His followers beyond the letter of the law and shows how they are to live in internal obedience to God. Specifically, the Beatitudes are well-known foundations for Christian spirituality. If we're going to be Christian, these are the *attitudes* that should *be* evident in our lives.

CHAPTER 9

The Upside-down Kingdom

by Reuben Welch

THE TITLE FOR THIS CHAPTER is the right one. The words of Jesus in the Beatitudes turn everything upside down. Or maybe right side up! The "blesseds" are so familiar we have forgotten how revolutionary they are. They are not simply wonderful words that begin the Sermon on the Mount. They are wonderful, all right, but they are also radical in their subversion of the values of our culture and our ordinary lives. They are sacred paradoxes that contradict the way the world works and at the same time bear the promise that the way God works will be the way the world works when "the kingdom of the world has become the kingdom of our Lord and of his Christ, and he will reign for ever and ever" (Revelation 11:15).

At the close of the Sermon on the Mount (Matthew 5—7) Jesus said that if we would hear His words and do them, our lives would be secure no matter what. Yet if we hear them without doing them, we will finally experience disaster (7:24-27). It is as simple as that. So our purpose is clear: receive the Beatitudes as from Jesus himself, respond to them in trust and obedience, and be blessed.

Blessed

The Sermon on the Mount (and remember, it is a sermon preached and not a law passed) begins with that wonderful word "blessed." It is a good word. Some versions have "Happy are the . . ."; others translate the word, "Oh the happiness of . . ." I think "happiness" would be a good translation if we could free it from our common, worldly, shallow understanding and give it depth and meaning in relation to God. It expresses the deep inward joy of those who wait on God and trust His promise for final salvation and who experience even now the reality of His saving presence.

"Blessed Are the Poor in Spirit . . ."

Poor people have no power or influence in society. They have no real independence or ability to determine their own future. Their hope must be in someone or something beyond themselves. In this startling beatitude, Jesus puts himself on the side of such people. Those who are poor in spirit are those who, like other poor people, know that they have no resources in themselves and must trust in God. People who have reached the bottom know they must have help. We need to know that about ourselves and to live without any pretending before God and in total dependence upon Him. We are blessed because full dependence upon God means that God's resources become our resources. These are hard, upside-down words because the goal of our culture is to be self-sufficient, self-starting, self-directing, and independently self-fulfilled. Jesus contradicts all this self-deceit and takes His place beside those who feel their personal failure and inadequacy, who are poor before God and trust Him and not themselves. The Kingdom belongs to them in the sense that they receive and live under the kingly rule of God and under the blessings of heaven.

My grandfather, known as Uncle Buddy Robinson, was a well-known and remarkably effective evangelist in his generation. On his deathbed he, talking aloud to himself and to God, thinking, I'm sure, of his long life of ministry, said over and over, "Just a pile of filthy rags." That's an image from Isaiah 64:6 in the King James Version he loved and memorized: "all our righteousnesses are as filthy rags." No wonder he was blessed! His trust was not in himself but in God. Consequently, his resources were not limited to himself but to the God of no limits.

"Blessed Are Those Who Mourn . . ."

I don't think this beatitude can stand alone like a proverb. Those who mourn fill the earth. Half of our TV news images are nameless faces of mourning people, grieving over dead and dying loved ones. They are hardly blessed. Neither are we blessed as we watch with casual interest the terrible atrocities revealed to us by reporters who seem totally dispassionate and objective.

We know that mourning is not necessarily good in itself; suffering turns as many people to bitterness as to God. On the other hand, we must say that some values are found in suffering that we don't seem to discover any other way. What if no one mourned or felt sorrow or remorse? It would be a world without compassion, a world of neither love nor joy. Still, it is not mourning as such that is blessed. Who, then, are the blessed and comforted mourners?

This beatitude can never make sense apart from Jesus. He is the one who *can* say that mourners are blessed. He is the one who *does* say it—to us personally. I believe that the mourning of this beatitude comes from the inevitable pain of being poor in spirit before God. As long as we close off our feelings and withhold ourselves from the light of God's judging, healing grace, we can go on our superficially happy way. So long as we hold back from being vulnerable to each other or maintain insensitivity to the real hurts and pains of the world, we can live quite contentedly. However when we let God show us our hearts and when we let ourselves feel the hurt and pain of others, we mourn. Mourning is the spirit of repentance before God, the spirit of a broken and contrite heart that grieves over what our failures have done and mourns for all that could have been. It is one thing to say, "We're all human, no one's perfect." It is another thing to open our lives to examination in God's presence. That is the mourning that receives comfort. I wonder, do we ever truly experience the comfort of God if we never truly mourn our loss before Him?

The consummation promises us comfort, when sin and evil are done away and God wipes away every tear (Revelation 7:17). In the meantime, in our present condition, we know the consolation of Christ's presence by His Spirit; we share His companionship and daily receive His strength. That's a comfort.

"Blessed Are the Meek . . ."

The meek or gentle are very much like the poor in spirit. The beatitude is a near quote from Psalm 37:10-11. In the Old Testament, the meek or the gentle are the disenfranchised who are totally dependent upon God for help, who cannot vindicate themselves and wait expectantly for God to vindicate them when His rule becomes visible on earth. The Creator and the Lord of the land is their Master and Benefactor, so all the earth is theirs.

The problem with "meek" is that it sounds like "weak." Our mental image of a truly meek person is pathetic—usually a born loser or doormat type. I wish the word were "mong," because that sounds like "strong," and we have great need to be strong. I doubt they will change it. Another translation is "gentle," but that is not much better because it is the word we use for the way we handle a little baby. When we get a puppy for the children we say, "Be gentle, go easy!"

It helps me understand meekness to remember that two great Bible personalities were meek. One was Moses who "was very meek, more than all men that were on the face of the earth" (Numbers 12:3, RSV). Think of his life, his great stresses, and his great strength. He kept his head on straight because he had a very special relationship with God (Numbers 12:6-8). The other person was Jesus, who invited us who are weary and burdened down to come to Him for rest because He was "gentle and humble in heart" (Matthew 11:29). Think of His life and His great stresses and His great strength. He was able to keep His head on straight because He was totally dependent on His Father. I wish we could get unhinged from the mistaken notion that meekness is a personality trait. It does not mean no stress, no conflict, no struggle, no emotional upheaval. It is a posture toward God, a relationship of total dependence upon Him. We can be gentle in the arena of personal encounters if we know that God is in charge here and that we are in His care.

This turns everything upside down. Our society says that the ones who push and struggle, who seize the opportunity and are assertive, get the prize. No, they don't! This is our Father's world. We are His children living on His good earth now, and in the final renewal, it will be our sure and secure place to be in heaven (see 2 Corinthians 6:10; Revelation 21:1). Meantime, let's be gentle.

"Hunger and Thirst for Righteousness . . ."

"Righteousness" is a big word in Matthew's Gospel. Like salvation, it means peace, integrity, harmony, wholeness, health, social justice, and right relationships. *Shalom* may be a good synonym. First of all, righteousness is the gift of God of a new and right relationship with Him. It is a parallel word to *justification*. It is not our hopeless struggle to measure up and try hard to please God; it is the trusting acceptance of His offer of forgiving grace that brings us into personal, loving relationship with Him. God satisfies the heart that hungers and thirsts for such a relationship.

This relationship spills out into a lifestyle that is appropriate to people living in trustful and obedient relationship to God. So righteousness is goodness of life and character. It means living right, paying bills, living and dealing honestly, not a life of duplicity but of transparency and integrity.

And it means justice. It means vindication for those whose cause is just. It means justice for those who are suffering injustice because the law is weighted in favor of one class or one color, because the favored few have too much and far too many do not have enough. It means justice for those treated as property or things and not as persons in the image of God.

Jesus uses language that pictures a desperately hungry person longing for food or a thirsty person crying out for water. Maybe we have not because we ask not (James 4:2) or because we do not keep asking or seeking or knocking (Matthew 7:7-8; see also Luke 11:5-13; 18:1-8). Our passive attitude allows us to slide along without coming to terms with what is not right in our relationship with God or in the situations around us. With no burning desire for righteousness, our lifestyle gradually conforms to the ways of the world.

God cares about righteousness, cares that the right prevails. Do we? Are we thirsting and hungering for the triumph of God's good cause in us and in our world enough to do anything at all about it? The promise is sure. God's cause will endure, triumph, and satisfy the hunger of our hearts.

"Blessed Are the Merciful . . ."

The kingdom of God is a kingdom of right relationships. It is a family into which we come as forgiven. In it we are in a new relationship with God and a new relationship with each other. Only one thing keeps it going: mercy, repeated over and over again. It doesn't ever start with us. It starts with God. He is the merciful One. God's mercy is the wonderful way He keeps love and covenant with His people even when they don't do the same for Him.

Is there anything we need more in our violent culture than mercy toward each other? Yet it will never happen till we know that God is merciful toward us who do not deserve it. Only out of His mercy can we be loving and forgiving to others who do not deserve it. God has bound himself to us in covenant love, and we are bound to each other in the bonds of covenant love. So we extend mercy as we have received it. This is a hard thing, a thing that turns everything upside down. "Don't get mad, get even." Ever heard that? That is not God's way, and it is not our way as His children. Mercy is our way.

It is not only a feeling or a gentle attitude. The real illustration of mercy is Jesus' story of the Good Samaritan (Luke 10:30-37). Mercy spills out as kindness, forgiveness, forbearance, graciousness, and helpfulness. What a word! What a wonder that God is that way toward us in Jesus.

Jesus said that the merciful will receive mercy. This is no spiritual bargain with God. It is not "blessed are those who overlook the sins of others for theirs will be overlooked." Mercy is God's gift to us undeserving men and women. Yet how can we receive it if we are unforgiving and unmerciful? The elder brother in the familiar parable of the prodigal son (Luke 15) was unwilling to come to the party with his repentant brother. That attitude excluded him from the father's house. The door was open, and the father urged him to come in, but his own unforgiving spirit made it impossible.

We won't receive mercy at the Final Judgment because we have been kind. Actually, we will receive in full measure that mercy we experience now through the pardoning grace of Jesus.

"Blessed Are the Pure in Heart . . ."

This beatitude takes us to the central issue—what about our hearts? In the Bible, the heart is the center of the person, the innermost part. Maybe it is the person we talk to when we talk to ourselves honestly. It is the center of thinking, planning, and willing. "Above all else, guard your heart, for it is the wellspring of life" (Proverbs 4:23).

Two things impress me. One is, what we are in our hearts is what we are. The other is that any change in us that is significant must come from the heart. Yet our own hearts can't change us. Jesus said that our hearts are the source of our impurity (Matthew 15:19-20). Only God can cleanse and change our hearts. He looks on the heart and can purify our hearts (see 1 Samuel 16:7 and Acts 15:9).

Jesus was pure in heart. We see what a pure heart looks like by looking at Him. We see His single-minded loyalty to His Father, His utter openness and sincerity before Him, His trust and His obedience. That is what pure in heart is, and it involves the purging from our hearts of false loves, false loyalties, and divided affections. Kierkegaard's famous phrase is "Purity of heart is to will one thing." For Jesus it was to do the will of His Father.

Jesus was pure, and He did indeed see God. We, too, can be blessed in seeing God. We will see Him in the last day, see Him as He is, and so be like Him (1 John 3:2). That future vision is also our present reality. We see Him now in personal fellowship with Him. We see Him supremely in Jesus. And we see Him in each other. I wonder if that's the way we see God clearest of all, this side of heaven? (See 1 John 4:12.)

"Blessed Are the Peacemakers . . ."

What a beatitude for our time! The anger, hostility, enmity, hatred, and bitterness of our violent culture overwhelm us. Truth is, without peace we will destroy and be destroyed. Blessed, indeed, are those who make peace. Nevertheless, it is not an easy word. In our normal usage, "peace" means the absence of conflict. No war equals peace. The older we get, the more we want a peaceful life, which means a life without stress or disagreements, without confrontations. The problem is that when defined this way, peacemakers are peace *lovers*. They are tranquilizers who want to smooth things over and avoid conflict. Being a devout coward, I understand this point of view. Nevertheless we can cover our destructive situations and ignore vital issues and so perpetuate evil because we want to "keep peace."

The Bible has a different point of view. The Old Testament word for peace is *shalom*. It never means the absence of something but rather harmony, health, wholeness, right relationships, well-being—or salvation. God himself is the Author of peace, and Christ "is our peace" who "came and preached peace" (Ephesians 2:14-17). The peace of God is a positive thing. Not so much like silence as like the music of an orchestra. Not the peace of the cemetery but the wholeness of a real, live, loving family.

Peace lovers and peacemakers are not the same. Overcoming an enemy is easier than overcoming enmity. It is easier to stop a quarrel than to heal it. To be a peacemaker means to establish peace and harmony between persons— as any police officer who has tried to intervene in domestic violence will tell you. But we know that envy, strife, and discord are contrary to God's will. And we know that for Him and for us, the reconciling, healing process is costly. The One who is our peace made "peace through his blood, shed on the cross" (Colossians 1:20).

We are called to be peacemakers. It is costly for us, too, but it is good to know our purpose as Christians in our families, churches, neighborhoods, and places of work. We are to be agents of reconciliation and instruments of peace—to work it out, talk it out, keep it up until harmony reigns. That is the task of folks like us who are privileged in grace to be children of God.

"Blessed Are the Persecuted . . ."

It is good that this beatitude follows the previous one. Peacemakers are likely to be persecuted. Actually, this beatitude is different from the others in that it refers not to what the followers of Jesus are or do but to what happens to them in the world.

Most of us don't know much about persecution in a violent or severe sense. Yet there are Christians who are alone in their families. I think of those who come to church without husbands or wives. I think of young people who come without their parents, brothers or sisters. It might not exactly be persecution, but it doesn't miss by far.

Some work in environments that are either indifferent or antagonistic to our faith. They hear the comments and sense the rejection or disdain, bear with vulgar and unclean language, and it hurts. Our faith puts us in awkward situations with neighbors and friends when our lifestyles and theirs are different, yet we want to be friends and be sociable. It is not a simple thing—and not without pain as we try to do the right thing situation by situation.

When we align ourselves with Jesus, we leave the world's perspective and come over on His side. Thus we pick up the rejection that the world has for Jesus. Yet Jesus says that we are blessed. The world rejects Jesus and so rejects us. That rejection puts Him and us together! There is a wonderful change in the last part of this beatitude that illustrates this. In verse 10, the persecution is for righteousness' sake, and in verse 11, Jesus says, "because of me." We are not identified with a cause, even a righteous cause. We are identified with Him and He with us. We are joined with Jesus in mind and heart. To pick up the cost of siding with Him is a blessed thing.

The Law and the Prophets

Matthew 5:17-20 is a difficult paragraph because it sounds as if Jesus has suddenly gone back to the law. He came preaching the gospel of the Kingdom. All through His ministry He was criticized for not keeping all the dos and don'ts of the legal system. Yet here He says that even the tiny letters and markings of the law will not pass away until all is fulfilled. We need to do and teach the commandments, even the least, if we would have any greatness in the kingdom of heaven. Has Jesus temporarily become a legalist?

I think the answer is in this word: "I tell you that unless your righteousness surpasses that of the Pharisees and the teachers of the law, you will certainly not enter the kingdom of heaven" (5:20). This greater righteousness must be supremely important! What is it? Well, we know for sure what it is *not*. The scribes and Pharisees had been keeping the whole legal system, down to the last dot. Yet Jesus said that we have to do better than that, or we won't even get in the door. The problem is that we have to keep the law, but we can't keep the law. For sure, we can't keep it better than they did!

Something here has to be turned upside down. That is just what Jesus does. He did not come to scrap the law because the law was the expression of the will and purposes of God. God's purpose for the law was fulfilled in Jesus' life, His love, His grace in healing, forgiving, and restoring. By His own obedient life Jesus fulfilled the law, and by His teaching He reinterpreted it in terms of love—His love. Love fulfills the law (see Matthew 22:35-40; Romans 13:8-10). Our obedience to the law, then, is obedience in love to Jesus and His teaching. It is the love of Jesus lived out by loving our brothers and sisters. So we don't scrap the law either, we fulfill it as we love the Lord with all our hearts and our neighbors as ourselves (Matthew 22:37-40). This is what the "greater righteousness" is.

Our trust is in Jesus. He is our Interpreter, our Teacher. His Spirit is the inspiration and power of our obedience; His will, the joy of our lives as we seek to live out His law of love. This is what turns the Kingdom right side up!

About the author: Reuben Welch, Ph.D., is retired chaplain and professor emeritus of religion at Point Loma Nazarene College in San Diego, California.

John 19—20

INTRODUCTION

Now we turn to the part of the story of salvation that is at the same time grim and glorious. John has to tell us about Jesus' trial and His death by crucifixion. This is the focal point of the story of salvation: Jesus—the One who is both God and man—hanging on a Roman cross to pay for our sins.

We must walk through the grim days of the story to understand how Jesus suffered. We must look at the cruel attempt by the powers of the world to silence God's message Jesus came to bring. We must gaze upon the Master, dead and buried, before we get to the real climax of the story—the Resurrection.

Specifically the empty tomb witnesses to the fact that the resurrection of Christ had physical aspects. If we truly believe that God performed the stupendous act of raising Jesus from the dead, we will not quibble about how He could or could not have done it. The bodily resurrection of the Lord is theologically very important in showing that the whole of creation is to be redeemed, the physical no less than the spiritual.*

We cannot leave out the Resurrection from our look at salvation history. Though the details leading up to it are grim, the resurrection of Jesus is a glorious chapter in salvation history.

---

*Leon Morris, *The Gospel According to John* (Grand Rapids, Mich.: Wm. B. Eerdmans Publishing Co., 1971), 829-30.

CHAPTER *10*

A Tree and a Grave

by Michael Lodahl

WHEN WE READ ABOUT JESUS' ARREST, trial, crucifixion, and resurrection in the Gospel of John, by far the most important truth to keep in mind is this: For John, *Jesus is the portrait of God at work in His world.*

What an amazing truth this is! John's profound conviction that God has made himself known in Jesus is at the root of his further confession that "God is love" (1 John 4:8, 16). This confession is probably the most fundamental of Christian beliefs about God.

In the Wesleyan tradition of Christian faith, we have understood *self-giving love* to be the very heart of God. How did John the beloved disciple say it? "This is how we know what love is: Jesus Christ laid down his life for us. And we ought to lay down our lives for [one another]" (1 John 3:16).

Jesus, God's Living Parable

Thus, when we turn to the Gospel of John's treatment of Jesus' passion, we understand that we are to read it as a *living parable,* a flesh-and-blood enactment of God's love in, and for, the world (see 3:16). If John defined love as Jesus laying down His life for us, then indeed in chapters 19 and

20 of his Gospel, we see the human portrait of God's love in action.

This is not simply amazing; it is revolutionary! This portrait of God's sacrificial, suffering love presents a radical challenge to most of our assumptions about God. It is not unusual to find people assuming that God is like a stern or even abusive parent. Or that God is like a police officer who swings a heavy billy club. Or that God is like a mighty king who rules His lowly subjects with little care for their hardships. Or even that God is an all-powerful manipulator who moves helpless people around like chess pieces. However, what happens to such popular assumptions when we begin with John's conviction that *God is like Jesus?*

We begin to see that God does not force himself upon us. "He came to that which was his own, but his own did not receive him" (John 1:11). We find that God's love flows well beyond social and cultural conventions. Jesus spoke freely of the "living water" with a despised Samaritan woman and with her whole village (4:1-42). We discover that even religious sanctions (like Sabbath observance), important as they were to Jewish identity, take a backseat to God's compassion for suffering human beings (5:1-11; 9:1-41). We learn that human tears and sorrow deeply move God, even to the point of weeping with those who weep (11:33-39). We find, in short, *a God who lavishly gives himself to us* in the passionate love of Jesus Christ.

Such news seems almost too good to be true. Certainly it was beyond Pilate's capacity to believe. When confronted by Jesus' testimony about the truth of God—the testimony that Jesus' very life provided—Pilate responded, probably cynically, "What is truth?" (18:38). Pilate, representing the politics of worldly power, was finally dumbfounded by the likes of Jesus. He asked, "Where do you come from?" (19:9). Earlier the Pharisees, representing the politics of religious power, responded to the testimony of Christ in frustration and anger. "We are disciples of Moses!

We know that God spoke to Moses, but as for this fellow, we don't even know where he comes from" (9:28-29). Neither the Roman nor the Jewish centers of authority could figure out "where Jesus was coming from."

Where does Jesus come from? This was the issue as John turned toward that final weekend of Jesus' earthly ministry, a weekend that occupies nearly half of John's Gospel. In chapter 13 John gave us his version of Jesus' final, climactic supper with His disciples. We read that "Jesus knew that the Father had put all things under his power, and that *he had come from God* and was returning to God" (v. 3, emphasis added). It is absolutely crucial for us to see that John says that *precisely because Jesus knew these things,* "he got up from the meal, took off his outer clothing, and wrapped a towel around his waist . . . and began to wash his disciples' feet" (vv. 4-5). Having come from God, Jesus portrays God as One who is a Servant, so humble as to be willing to wash dirty, human feet—including the feet of a traitor.

Is it any wonder that neither the Roman nor the Jewish authorities could accept that where Jesus came from was God? Such a God as this upsets all traditional notions of divine and earthly power. Such a God challenges the securities of prestige. After all, if the mighty God of all creation reveals His power and authority by getting on His knees and washing feet, then truly the kingdoms of this world are weighed in the balance and found wanting.

The Suffering God

On "the day of Preparation of Passover Week, about the sixth hour" (19:14), or around noon on Passover eve— the very hour when the Temple priests would have been preparing Passover lambs for slaughter—Jesus was taken to the hill of Golgotha to be crucified. Ironically, though the Jewish chief priests were denying Jesus' innocence and calling for His death (19:15-16), they were at the same time, in fact, preparing the Passover Lamb for sacrifice, "the Lamb of God, who takes away the sin of the world" (1:29; see also 1 Corinthians 5:7-8).

Surely it is difficult for us today, with crosses adorning our church steeples and shining beautifully in our stained-glass windows, to appreciate the horror of the Roman execution stake. Our Gospels do not go into the grisly details, and neither need we. Suffice it to say that crucifixion was a horrid, slow, and utterly humiliating way to die. Battered and naked, bloody and entirely vulnerable, stretched out upon the Cross, Jesus opens up to us the very suffering heart of the eternal God!

Jesus' Words from the Cross

We know from descriptions of crucifixion scenes in secular sources of the time that they usually brought out the worst in people. Roman soldiers would often revel in sadistic violence toward their prisoners—as they certainly did with Jesus (19:1-5). However, often the lust of blood would then spread to the gathered onlookers, who would taunt or even further torture the helpless and vulnerable victims. History describes those who were crucified as having been in terrible agony, often shrieking in pain or cursing their torturers with ugly blasphemies.

Knowing this makes Jesus' crucifixion all the more remarkable. For here we do not encounter one who curses and blasphemes. Instead we see One who, even in such agony of body and spirit, still expresses concern for others rather than himself.

Later, Jesus said simply, "I am thirsty." Long, painful exposure in the midday Judean sun would have caused extreme dehydration. Many centuries prior, David the psalmist had lamented, "My strength is dried up like a potsherd, and my tongue sticks to the roof of my mouth" (Psalm 22:15). Jesus could relate. The thirst He experienced was real human thirst.

John's Gospel is the only one to tell us that Jesus accepted something to drink. He sipped from a sponge soaked with "wine vinegar" (19:29), which was a weak, diluted drink of the Roman soldiers. It should not be confused with another drink, the "wine mixed with myrrh" mentioned in Mark 15:23, which Jesus refused to drink. That particular drink was a narcotic sedative that charitable Jewish women would mix and offer to crucifixion victims. Jesus chose to undergo this most horrid of deaths with a clear head. In fact, the drink that Jesus received could have done nothing more than temporarily quench His thirst— and thus sustain or even heighten His awareness.

Upon receiving the drink, Jesus spoke His last words from the Cross, as far as John's Gospel is concerned: "It is finished" (19:30). These are not the words of a despairing man who has come to the end of his rope. Rather, these are the words of One who knows that He has now fulfilled His purpose for coming into the world (see 12:27 and 19:28). Jesus, the Lamb of God, poured out His lifeblood for our sins. As John wrote later, "the blood of Jesus, [God's] Son, purifies us from all sin" (1 John 1:7). "It is finished!" is the cry of triumph of the Suffering Savior from a Roman cross that, as far as the world is concerned, signifies nothing but weakness, humiliation, and death. Yet the Cross is, in truth, the very instrument of God's salvation of the world.

The Triumph of God over Death

It is important for us to understand that Jesus really did die. To deny that Jesus either could or did die would be to deny that Jesus truly shared in our human condition. This is why John's Gospel and later Christian confessions such as the Apostles' Creed go to such pains to insist that Jesus was dead and buried. No life remained in that brutalized body the Romans took down from the Cross. From all human appearances, the politics of worldly and religious power had won the day.

Yet as John's Gospel insists repeatedly, God speaks a word of judgment against those worldly systems of power and authority—and that Word is Jesus. Beyond human sin, cruelty, and violence, beyond death, the grave, and hell itself, God has the last Word.

It was not the empty tomb, however, that assured the disciples of Christ's victory over death. Rather, the utterly mysterious and entirely unexpected appearances of Jesus—alive once again—rekindled their faith. It is worth noting that John's Gospel echoes the other Gospels' testimonies about resurrection appearances. Jesus first appeared to women, whose opinions in religious matters were neither encouraged, respected, nor heeded in first-century Palestine.

Mary Magdalene had been there at the foot of Jesus' cross, beholding in horror her Lord and Teacher as He slowly and painfully died (see 19:25). No wonder she did not recognize Him immediately, for Jesus would have been just about the last person she'd have expected to meet in the burial garden. Yet when He spoke her name, like a good shepherd who "calls his own sheep by name and leads them out" (10:3), Mary recognized her Living Lord.

His response to her enthusiastic greeting seems to have signaled a crucial change in the nature of Jesus' relationship to His followers. "Do not hold on to me," Jesus said to Mary, "for I have not yet returned to the Father" (20:17). In effect He was saying, "Do not cling to me as though you could keep me in your grasp." He was beginning to wean His disciples away from the physically oriented relationship to Him that had been typical under the conditions of everyday life. Instead, they had now to begin to understand and experience the Living Christ as a profoundly *spiritual* reality, as the One who was returning to the Father.

Jesus' resurrection, however, did not undo or negate His human existence or experience. Nor did it erase His profound sense of kinship to His disciples. Indeed, His words to Mary were, "Go instead to my brothers and tell them, 'I am returning to my Father and your Father, to my God and your God'" (20:17). Even as our resurrected and glorious Lord today, Jesus still calls us His brothers and sisters. Indeed, He invites us to call *His* Father "our Father" even as He humbles himself to call *our* God His God. Truly, we have One who represents us in heavenly places.

Christ's Church, Heir of the Spirit's Breath of Life

John's telling of that first Easter evening has a beauty that lingers down through the centuries, for it yet tells us what it is like for us to be in the presence of the Living Christ.

John offers first that Jesus brings His peace to our troubled and fearful hearts. "[Shalom] Peace be with you!" Jesus said twice to His shocked disciples (20:19, 21). It was the standard greeting of that culture, but it was more than simply a greeting. Jesus' living presence *brings* peace. Indeed, He *is* our peace. He has broken down every wall— the walls between God and humanity, between male and female, rich and poor, Jew and Greek, White and Black, Asian and Hispanic. Peace!

Our son Bryan, when he was younger, usually had two items at the top of his bedtime prayer list: "no nightmares" and "no spiders to get me." His mother and I certainly honored his prayer requests. Nevertheless, we concluded every prayer with the traditional Hebrew blessing: "The LORD bless you and keep you; the LORD make his face shine upon you and be gracious to you; the LORD turn his face toward you and give you peace" (Numbers 6:24-26). By the time we would reach that final benediction of peace, it was far more than a nice wish or hopeful prayer. Instead, we had *bestowed* peace upon our little one. As Bryan would close his eyes for sleep, we always knew that nightmares and spiders were not quite so threatening as they had been only a few minutes before. If a parent can bestow such peace upon a child in a bedtime blessing, how much more can our Heavenly Father's Son bestow peace upon us and within us by His very presence?

It is not incidental to Jesus' blessing that between His two greetings of shalom to this frightened little bunch, He offered them His hands and side. His scars did not simply provide evidence that it truly was Jesus in their midst. Those scars also signified, even today, the wounded nature of the eternal, resurrection body of the Living Christ. He still bears those wounds. We are, as it were, engraved in the palms of His hands. The resurrection of Jesus did not lift Him beyond His passion in such a way to forever erase its evidences. No, Jesus yet bears His scars, a living parable of the God who knows, understands, and shares in our pains.

Only when we have heard and felt that peace that the living Christ bestows upon us are we ready for His commission, "As the Father has sent me, I am sending you" (20:21). Earlier, we considered the mystery of God's humble love revealed in Jesus' act of washing His disciples' feet. Now, however, we remember that He followed it with, "Now that I, your Lord and Teacher, have washed your feet, you also should wash one another's feet" (13:14). He went on that evening to teach them, "As the Father has loved me, so have I loved you. Now remain in my love" (15:9). The same sending, loving, obeying, and abiding that characterize the Son's relationship to the Father are now to characterize our relationship to the Son. Just as we encounter God in Christ, so in us, others encounter the Living Christ. We are called to be part of a chain reaction of redemptive love that began in the boundless, eternally loving heart of God, proceeded out of the bosom of the Father, became flesh among us, and now flows into our lives by the Spirit.

The Living, yet wounded, Christ offers us His peace and sends us out to be His ambassadors. Like His first band of disciples, we cannot go out to be His witnesses without inhaling the fresh breath of His Spirit. For even now, Jesus breathes upon us and says, "Receive the Holy Spirit" (20:22). When we receive the Spirit, we receive life—the divine life of peace and love.

The Holy Spirit is the Spirit of life. Remember that it was the Spirit of God who brooded over the surface of the chaotic waters in Genesis 1. Recall that in Genesis 2 "the LORD God formed the man from the dust of the ground and breathed into his nostrils the breath of life, and the man became a living being" (v. 7). Keep in mind the prophet Ezekiel who prophesied over the dry and bleached bones in the valley of Israel's desolation and how the Spirit-breath of God restored and renewed those bones to life (Ezekiel 37:1-14). No wonder the prayer of Christ's Church throughout the centuries has been, "Come, Creator Spirit, and renew us!"

I get severe headaches every so often. One of the ways the doctor has helped me to keep them under control is by having me breathe from a tank of pure oxygen when I feel a migraine coming on. Of course I'm always breathing oxygen, but the plain stuff we breathe most of the time doesn't clean out my head. In fact, it may be part of what ails me. Still, that pure oxygen really heals the headaches! Similarly, the Spirit is always giving us Christians life, always sustaining and nurturing us, almost like the air we breathe—and yet at times we may need an inhalation of "pure oxygen." We may need a fresh infilling of the Spirit to clear the cobwebs, to heal us, to restore us to spiritual vitality. Just as surely as He stood in the midst of His frightened disciples, so also the Living Christ stands in our midst today and breathes upon us. May we be ready and open to receive His holy breath!

About the author: Michael Lodahl, Ph.D., is professor of religion at Northwest Nazarene College in Nampa, Idaho.

Romans 6—8

INTRODUCTION

In our journey along the time line of salvation history, we come to a passage that brings us to a deep and important question: How can we be free from the struggle with sin?

It is a reality that when we commit our lives to following the teachings of the Savior, we find an intense internal strife trying to draw us away from Him. The apostle Paul wrestled with this and wrote honestly of the struggle.

The Book of Romans is a letter written by Paul to the Christians who lived in Rome. Paul probably wrote Romans in the early spring of A.D. 57. It is likely Paul was on his third missionary journey and ready to return to Jerusalem. He sent this letter to prepare the Roman Christians for his visit and proposed mission to Spain. In the Epistle he presented the basic theology of salvation to a congregation that had not been taught by an apostle. In addition, Paul "sought to explain the relationship between Jews and Gentiles in God's overall plan of redemption. The Jewish Christians were being rejected by the larger Gentile group in the church because the Jewish believers still felt constrained to observe dietary laws and sacred days."*

In our review of salvation history, today we focus on chapters 6, 7, and 8. These chapters deal in depth with the primary question of Holiness churches: How can we live holy lives when our human tendency seems to be to continue sinning? Do we adhere more rigidly to rules so we will feel pure? Or do we learn to love the One who truly can make us free? When we have answered those questions as Paul did, we have the means to live victoriously and follow in the steps of our Savior.

The NIV Study Bible, ed. Kenneth Barker (Grand Rapids, Mich.: Zondervan Publishing House, 1985), 1703.

CHAPTER *11*

Winning the Battle with Sin

by William M. Greathouse

"OUR BELOVED BROTHER PAUL," Simon Peter said, "wrote . . . some things . . . hard to understand, which the ignorant and unstable twist to their own destruction" (2 Peter 3:15-16).[1]

Among these hard-to-understand things is Paul's doctrine of justification with which Romans 6 begins. Understood properly, this doctrine opens the door to a life of victory over sin, but someone can misunderstand it as a license for sinning. In Paul's own day his critics were twisting this teaching to mean, "If my sinning elicits from God the manifestation of His righteousness, as Paul claims, then why should I not go on sinning?" (see 3:5-7). A natural conclusion would be, "Let us do evil so that good may come" (3:8).

However, this misunderstanding of Paul's gospel of free grace was not simply a problem of the New Testament church. A recent book from a major religious publisher, *Sin Boldly—Trust God More Boldly!* takes its cue from Luther who, as Wesley rightly said, was clear on justification but "confused" on sanctification. This confusion is widespread in Protestant circles.

The Beginning of Our Sanctification

Romans 6 is a powerful declaration that justification is the *beginning* of our sanctification. It opens, however, with

Paul letting his critics state their objection to his doctrine. If, as Paul has just stated, justification is by faith alone, apart from works of the law; and if the law, rather than making possible a holy life, serves only to make sin abound; and if where sin abounded, grace abounded all the more (5:18-21), "Should we continue to sin in order that grace may abound?" (6:1).

"By no means!" Paul shouted. "How can we who died to sin go on living in it?" (6:2). "What ghastly logic!" Paul is saying. "How can we as Christians go on *living* in sin, since we as Christians have *died* to sin?"

When we come to Christ to be saved, we accept *His* death, making it our very own—His death *for* our sin becomes our death *to* sin. If we have really died and risen with Christ, how can we even *think* of sinning? Such a death to sin is what Paul meant, reinforcing his position by reminding his readers that by being baptized they had made this very profession.

According to Paul, baptized believers are professing that they are no longer the same persons as they once were. Baptism dramatically symbolizes our death, burial, and resurrection with Christ (6:3-4).

One of the strongest Christians of my acquaintance was once an alcoholic in his community. His coming to Christ revolutionized his life and broke the power of drink. "Whenever I'm tempted to go back to my old life," he once told me, "the memory of my baptism holds me true."

Now look at verses 5-11 of chapter 6 where the apostle spelled out the consequences of our death and resurrection with Christ:

- The first consequence is that "our old self" has been crucified with Christ so that our bodies are no longer under the control of sin (v. 6). The compulsion to sinning has been broken, "for whoever has died is freed from sin" (v. 7). Guilt gives sin its power over us. So, when the guilt of sin is dissolved, its power is broken.

"He breaks the pow'r of cancelled sin; / He sets the pris'ner free."[2]

- The second consequence follows: Christ not only died, but now He lives to God. So do we! He, unconditionally; we, conditionally. With Paul we confess, "I died to the law [my efforts to please God by my own works], so that I might live to God. I have been crucified with Christ; and it is no longer I who live, but it is Christ who lives in me" (Galatians 2:19-20).

Paul's conclusion was, "So you also must consider yourselves dead to sin and alive to God in Christ Jesus" (Romans 6:11). The verb "consider" does not denote pretending; rather, it indicates a deliberate and sober judgment based on faith in what God has done for us through Christ. If, *in fact,* we are in union with the crucified/resurrected Christ Jesus, we are, *in fact,* dead to sin and alive to God. His death is our death to sin. His life is our life to holiness. For one whose life is centered in Christ Jesus, this is life's deepest certainty.

In 6:12-14 Paul noted that although we may have died to sin, sin itself is not dead. It threatens our new existence in Christ. However, Paul added, by God's grace we are able *not* to sin. Just the same, our bodily desires, if not disciplined in the Spirit (see 8:12-13), may lead to sin (see James 1:14-15)—and once again to sin's dominion over us.

There is more here. Paul was calling for a moral showdown that will decide the question, "Who is in charge of my life, God or self?" "Present yourselves . . . and . . . your members to God," Paul urged in 6:13, employing a Greek tense demanding decisive action. In the final analysis, each of us is part either of God's problem or of God's solution. The call is for moral decision. Paul rephrased his appeal in 6:19: "I am speaking in human terms because of your natural limitations. For just as you once presented your members as slaves to impurity and to greater and greater iniquity, so now present your members as slaves to righteousness for sanctification."

Paul's call was for all-out abandonment to God and righteous living. He was addressing the deeper sin that we need to deal with—lurking *self-power* or deciding how much of our hearts God can have. Let our answer be, "Not just a part or half of my heart; I will give *all* to Thee."[3] When God has *all,* then our lives prove Paul's claim: "Sin will have no dominion over you, since you are not under law but under grace" (6:14).

However, even after we have settled the matter of who's in charge, victory over sin is not automatic. It never is. Victory is not a never-changing state. It is a condition, *a relationship with God maintained by obedience.* Listen to Paul: "You are slaves of the one whom you obey, either of sin, which leads to death, or of obedience, which leads to righteousness" (6:16).

Sin, here, clearly means willful disobedience, which opens the door to the reassertion of sin's control over us. Paul was not thinking of what John Wesley calls "sins of surprise" when in an unguarded moment we fail. By the grace of God, we need not sin. Paul was warning against something different—the false presumption that grace automatically covers known sin in the Christian life. He was trying to squash once and for all any suggestion that the gospel tolerates sin. He was warning the Christian, says one theologian, that one act of deliberate sin "might have the effect of placing the believer once again on the inclined plane which leads to the abyss."[4] Romans 6:23 was not intended as a text for an evangelistic sermon—it was the apostle's final warning that "the wages of sin is death." But, thank God, "the free gift of God is eternal life in Christ Jesus our Lord."

Helplessness Over Indwelling Sin

For many Christians, what the apostle had just said about victory over sin in Romans 6 seems to be overturned by what he went on to acknowledge in Romans 7:14-25. There he lamented his helplessness in the face of indwelling sin.

To make this passage a description of the normal Christian life is to violate the first principle of reading Scripture by isolating the passage from its context. Paul had just written that "sin will have no dominion over you, since you are not under law but under grace" (6:14). He went on to declare that "the law of the Spirit of life in Christ Jesus has set you free from the law of sin and of death" (8:2). How then, in this agonizing passage that does not even mention the Holy Spirit and refers to Christ only in a cry for deliverance, can Paul be understood as depicting *normal* Christian experience? If 7:14-25 is the normal Christian life, where is Christ superior to Moses? The apostle's purpose in this passage was to show *the powerlessness of the law to give victory over sin.*

The best Bible scholars today see Paul describing the moral and/or religious dilemma of *any human being* who does not know the victory over sin and self promised by the gospel of Christ. Paul knew what we all know most deeply about ourselves—by nature we are continually inclined to evil (see Genesis 6:5). Original sin is an observable fact. Inevitably, when we reach the age of moral accountability, we find ourselves succumbing to the "sin that dwells within [us]" (7:17).

Speaking for each of us, Paul said, "I am of the flesh, sold into slavery under sin" (v. 14). Yet not all that is within us is sinful. We also have minds that recognize the law of God (whether or not we acknowledge it as such) and its claims upon our consciences. Still, the mind is unable of itself to resist the seductive power of sin. "So I find it to be a law that when I want to do good, evil lies close at hand" (v. 21). Paul here used the term "law" to mean a "law of experience." He spoke for us all when, as a person without the sanctifying grace of the Spirit, he confessed, "I delight in

117

he law of God in my inmost self, but I see in my members another law at war with the law of my mind, making me captive to the law of sin [the sin-principle] that dwells in my members" (vv. 22-23).

Dutch Reformer James Arminius spoke of these two verses as "the war of laws." The law of God and the law of sin are at war with one another. In the same way, the law of our minds wages war against the law of our members.

Paul described the human dilemma when he said, "Wretched man that I am! Who will rescue me from this body of death?" (v. 24) "Jesus Christ our Lord!" Paul shouted in verse 25. The One who brings "the war of laws" to an end by introducing "the law of the Spirit of life in Christ Jesus" (8:2), a dynamic principle supplying what the law of God could never provide.[5]

Verse 25 of chapter 7 is Paul's conclusion. "So then, with my mind I [I of myself, RSV] am a slave to the law of God, but with my flesh I am a slave to the law of sin." This statement is the sum of what Paul had been saying in this passage. Coming after his shout of victory, it seems out of place. Nevertheless, as one author points out, "It is the expression of exultation that is out of place, but only because Paul could not contain himself longer."[6]

"I of myself" is the key to understanding the dilemma. The phrase signifies, "I, left to myself" (MOFFATT), "I relying on myself" (A. M. Hunter) to do the will of God. *False self-reliance is the last ditch stand of the carnal mind.* Thus, while 7:14-15 primarily describes the awakened sinner, it has an echo in the life of the unsanctified believer. Thank God, "there remaineth therefore a rest to the people of God" (Hebrews 4:9, KJV)—a rest from this inward battle with sin.

Romans 7:14-25, therefore, does not overthrow what Paul said in chapter 6. The apostle wrote Romans 7 to refute those who might believe that observing the law of God achieves victory over sin. This disputed passage simply shows the inability of the law to sanctify. Holiness is not the achievement of our human endeavor, no matter how sincere or intense. It is the gift of God to those who have come to the end of themselves and are ready to receive the sanctifying Spirit. This point is where Paul had been leading us all along.

No Longer Condemned

The grand announcement of Romans 8 is, "There is therefore now no condemnation [either from God or conscience] for those who are in Christ Jesus. For the law of the Spirit of life in Christ Jesus has set [us] free from the law of sin and of death" (8:1-2). Just as an aircraft is set free from the law of gravity by the law of aerodynamics, "the war of laws" is over. Christ Jesus has won the victory. As the incarnate Son of God, He met sin on its own territory (in human flesh) and there "condemned sin in the flesh" (8:3).

The battle may be continuing in a person's life, *but the war has been won*. Winning the battle with sin is not a matter of intense effort on our part, however sincere. Rather, it is a matter of resting in Christ Jesus, who has pronounced the doom of sin. He offers us the all-sufficient power of the Holy Spirit to lift us out of the flesh into a life in the Spirit.

First, the love of God flooding our hearts by the Holy Spirit (see 5:5) fulfills "the just requirement of the law" (8:4). What is that "just requirement"? Paul declared that "love is the fulfilling of the law" (13:10). He was not saying that *we* meet the law's requirement, as if we generate within ourselves the love that God desires. Instead, "the just requirement of the law [is] fulfilled *in* us" (8:4, emphasis added) by the Holy Spirit—a distinction that makes a profound difference in how we view and live our life in God.

Second, the Spirit not only fills our hearts with God's love, giving us an answering love that delights to do God's will, but also lifts our existence from the *flesh* into the *Spirit.* "The mind that is set on the flesh," Paul said, "is hostile to God [because it is self-centered]; it does not submit to

119

God's law—indeed it cannot, and those who are in the flesh cannot please God. *But you are not in the flesh; you are in the Spirit, since the Spirit of God dwells in you"* (8:7-9, emphasis added). In other words, the Spirit of God now exerts the same penetrative, controlling power once exerted by the sin that *formerly* dwelled in you.

Paul's next statement is highly significant: "Anyone who does not have the Spirit of Christ does not belong to him" (v. 9). "This," someone has said, "amounts to saying that all Christians 'have the Spirit' *in greater or lesser degree.*"[7] This "greater or lesser degree" of the Spirit's indwelling is a matter of *how yielded to God we are* (see 6:12-14, 19).

Another commentator writes,

> The Spirit-filled life, or Spirit-possessed life, is not one in which we have a certain amount of the Spirit, but rather in which He possesses all of us. The Spirit-filled life is one in which the Spirit expresses Himself within an individual as a controlling and overflowing force. The condition is one of yieldedness on our part. We are filled with the Spirit as we are emptied of self.[8]

Third, the Spirit-filled life is a matter of continued discipline in the Spirit (see 8:12-17). Paul's distinction between "flesh" and "body" is of prime importance. Here in Romans 7—8, "flesh" means "our fallen human existence" (as self-centered). When we have yielded ourselves to Christ and permitted Him to fill us with the Holy Spirit, we are "not in the flesh; [we] are in the Spirit" (8:9).

Yet we are still in bodies whose instincts, urges, and desires are clamoring only for fulfillment. Moreover, we are still humans with self-defense mechanisms. It was this body-self unit that Christ "came to seek out and to save" (Luke 19:10). Just the same, the "body" offers a point of attack for "flesh." Hence, Paul's warning, "If you live according to the flesh, you will die; *but if by the Spirit you put to death the deeds of the body, you will live"* (8:13, emphasis added). Living "by the Spirit" means a life of constant prayer and vigilance, minding the checks of the Spirit. It is a life of obedience. "If we walk in the light," said John, "as he himself is in the light, . . . the blood of Jesus his Son cleanses us from all sin" (1 John 1:7).

Finally, while we experience a continuous cleansing and maintain a Spirit-filled existence by walking in the light of God, our present life is one of "sufferings of this present time," as we await Christ's return to glorify our frail, burdensome bodies (8:18). Nevertheless, thank God, even now "the Spirit helps us in our weakness" (v. 26). Best of all, "we know that all things work together for good for those who love God, who are called according to his purpose" (v. 28). That purpose is that we "be conformed to the image of his Son, in order that he might be the firstborn within a large family" (v. 29).

The final majestic paragraph of Romans 8 is Paul's inspired conclusion, celebrating the glorious truth that we are *superconquerors* through Christ. Chapter 8, which began with "no condemnation," climaxes with no separation. Thank God, we will overcome—*to the glory of God alone!*

About the author: William M. Greathouse, Ph.D., is a retired general superintendent of the Church of the Nazarene and lives in Mount Juliet, Tennessee.

Notes

1. Unless otherwise indicated, all quotations in this chapter come from the New Revised Standard Version (NRSV).

2. Charles Wesley, "O for a Thousand Tongues to Sing," *Sing to the Lord* (Kansas City: Lillenas Publishing Co., 1993), 147.

3. Homer W. Grimes, "What Shall I Give Thee, Master?" *Special Voices* (Kansas City: Lillenas Publishing Co., 1964), 2.

4. Fredrick Godet, *St. Paul's Epistle to the Romans,* trans. A. Cusin (New York: Funk and Wagnalls, 1883), 262.

5. Carl Bangs, *Arminius: A Study of the Dutch Reformation* (Nashville: Abingdon Press, 1971), 188-92.

6. Donald M. Davis, "Freedom from the Law," *Interpretation: A Journal of Bible and Theology* 7 (April 1953): 162.

7. W. Sanday and H. C. Headlam, *The Epistle to the Romans,* in *The International Critical Commentary* (New York: Chas. Scribners Sons, 1929), 197 (italics added).

8. Myron Augsburger, *Quench Not the Spirit* (Scottsdale, Pa.: Herald Press, 1961), 39-40.

Philippians 2:5-13

INTRODUCTION

If we think about God's plan of salvation for any length of time, we will discover several amazing things. Human beings were lost creatures, having no means to save themselves. No amount of praying to deaf idols or creating human philosophies could change the bent toward destruction found in humans. Yet God, who could have let creation follow its own destructive choices, loved us so much He initiated steps to save us. He formulated the plan, took on human flesh, and fulfilled the plan. And He gave us enough instruction so that even the simplest among us can follow the way.

When we realize how amazing it is that God himself would become our Savior, we are moved to praise. How can we not shout praises of joy because of such a wonderful Savior? Our focal passage in this chapter of salvation history reveals Paul "singing" a hymn of praise about Christ.

Paul wrote the book called Philippians to the Christians in the town of Philippi. He wrote it from prison. Some believe that he was in prison in Ephesus around A.D. 53-55. Others think that the letter came from the Caesarean prison around A.D. 57-59. However, the best evidence places Paul, still in prison, at Rome in A.D. 61.

The Book of Philippians is a thank-you letter from the missionary Paul. In it he reports on the progress of his work. It also contains one of the most profound passages ever written about Christ.

The "Christ hymn" found in Philippians 2:5-11 is another natural stop along our review of salvation history. We can pause here and worship along with Paul because the hymn explains Jesus becoming the Savior in such a way as to inspire thankful worship and adoration in all Christians. When we understand what Paul is saying about Jesus, we have another chance to celebrate Christ in our hearts and in our lives.

CHAPTER 12

Being like Christ

by Morris A. Weigelt

PAUL'S LOVE FOR CHRIST and the salvation He brings is so deep and strong that he often breaks into poetic singing to try to capture the wonder and awe of it all. Philippians 2:5-11 is one of the most profound passages in the Bible. Even the earliest commentators recognized the hymnlike quality of the material. Simple prose is inadequate to capture the mystery of our relationship with our Lord.

Members of the Early Church focused their lives upon the understanding of their Lord. One writer described it this way:

> Everything of life was shared so the whole group could benefit, remember, learn, and sing together. In the sharing, remembering, learning, and singing, the story of Jesus became the story of the group. And so Jesus' character formed the group character. There was nothing of their life together that was not transformed by the story and presence of Christ among them.[1]

As Paul sang his praise to our Savior in this passage, we are invited to rehearse for ourselves the nature of our Lord—and to be transformed into that same image (see 2 Corinthians 3:18). The more complete the understanding of the character of the Messiah, the more both individual character and group character reflect the Master.

The Situation at Philippi

Paul had a wonderful relationship with the church at Philippi. Our records show that they were the only church he allowed to provide for him repeatedly. The warmth of that relationship is visible in every segment of the Epistle, this window into the very heart of the apostle.

However, friction in the church was evident. Some of the friction was external. (Check the clues in 1:18-30 and in chapter 3.) Some of the friction was internal. (Examine the opening of chapter 4.) Paul leads his friends at Philippi back to another look at the Savior to solve the disunity.

In the opening verses of chapter 2, he invites them to recognize the strengths they already have in order to bring them back to singing in harmony. The "if" clauses in verse one do not suggest any lack in their foundations. We could well translate the Greek "as a matter of fact, you already possess" these foundational virtues. You already possess a deep encouragement in Christ. You already own the consolation from love. You already are sharing in the work of the Spirit. Compassion and sympathy are already functioning in your midst. Since these common elements are already there, the harmony of the congregation as the Body of Christ should be the norm.

Note the variety of phrases Paul uses in 2:2-4 to speak of this way in which the model of Christ shapes the congregation: "of the same mind"; "the same love"; "being in full accord and of one mind"; no "selfish ambition or conceit"; "humility"; and "look . . . to the interests of others."[2] These are the normal indicators of a congregation shaped by the character of their Master.

The Character of the Master

Paul invites his readers to take another look at the Master as the model for their relationships. He has been writing beautifully as he makes the call to community, but now he really breaks forth into poetry. The passage reflects the flow and flair of the language by its very poetic structure in verses 5-11:

> Let the same mind be in you that was in Christ Jesus,
> who, though he was in the form of God,
>> did not regard equality with God
>> as something to be exploited,
> but emptied himself,
>> taking the form of a slave,
>> being born in human likeness.
> And being found in human form,
>> he humbled himself
>> and became obedient to the point of death—
>> even death on a cross.
> Therefore God also highly exalted him
>> and gave him the name
>> that is above every name,
> so that at the name of Jesus
>> every knee should bend,
>> in heaven and on earth and under the earth,
> and every tongue should confess
>> that Jesus Christ is Lord,
>> to the glory of God the Father.

The character of Christ that shapes the community of His followers is clearly visible in this hymn. That character is visible in the "mind . . . that was in Christ Jesus" (v. 5). The word "mind" refers to the total flow and direction of the personality. Our Lord had a total consistency of thought, emotion, will, and action.

Paul has no doubts about the deity of the Messiah. Verse 6 defines that equality with God that characterized Him. Paul writes first that Christ was in the "form of God." His divine character was fully visible in the Gospel records. He healed the sick, controlled nature, and forgave sins.

Paul is quick to note that His "equality with God" was not a privilege the Master chose to flaunt. No arrogance or manipulation of others grew out of His position as the Son. The writer to the Hebrews is careful to note that he grants the language of Sonship to Jesus because of His total obe-dience to the Father (5:8-9). The Gospel writers, John and Luke, record that total obedience in Jesus' own words. "The word that you hear is not mine, but is from the Father who sent me" (John 14:24). "The works that I do in my Father's name . . ." (John 10:25). "Yet, not my will but yours be done" (Luke 22:42).

Verses 7 and 8 of Philippians 2 use succinct, but powerful, language to speak of the humility and servanthood at the heart of the character of Jesus. Paul wrote of the voluntary "emptying" of the Master. He spoke of the servanthood in terms of human form and likeness. He wrote of an obedience that went beyond mere humility to the point of death itself. That death was no ordinary death—it was a cruel death on a hideous and painful Roman cross.

A number of writers noted the servanthood of our Lord—many of them echoing the 53rd chapter of Isaiah in which the prophet so movingly portrayed the Suffering Servant. John, for example, recorded that moment in the Upper Room when Jesus took the towel and the basin and washed the feet of the disciples. Service to His disciples was more significant than position for our Lord (see John 13:1-20).

Paul's hymn of adoration of the Lord moves beyond the obedient-servant theme to the exaltation theme in Philippians 2:9-11. God responds to His obedience by exalting Him—by giving Him the name that is above every name.

The confession of faith that "Jesus Christ is Lord" is no stammering creed. It is the recognition that the model of our Lord brings glory to the Father. It is the recognition that He understands our situation because of His total involvement in our world. He, and He alone, is worthy to be designated as Lord—the name that is above every name!

When we think of the character of our Lord and Master in these pictures, we are led to worship and adoration. Then we live out the principle that we become like the One whom we adore. Christlikeness is the normal pattern for those who continually offer worship and adoration to the Lord.

More than Just a Model

The model our Savior offers to us is beautiful and inspiring—and impossible to follow because of the ravages of sin in our lives and in our world. An inspiring model is not enough to create disciples and followers.

The death on the Cross, which Paul placed at the center of his hymn to the Messiah, points to the enabling He provides. That death on the Cross was not simply a beautiful example; it was an atoning death that purchased our salvation. In the opening prayer of chapter 1, Paul prayed that they will be "pure and blameless, having produced the harvest of righteousness that comes through Jesus Christ for the glory and praise of God" (vv. 10-11). In the third chapter, Paul made Christ his highest priority because of "the power of his resurrection" (v. 10).

The Servant has become the Savior. The death on the Cross purchased an atonement that cancels the hammerlock of sin upon our lives. The death of our Savior provides the power to live a life of servanthood and submission to the good of the community—even as He modeled servanthood in its most expensive manner.

The enabling that God alone has provided through the Cross accomplishes all of this. "For it is God who is at work in you, enabling you both to will and to work for his good pleasure" (2:13).

To sing with Paul this hymn of adoration to the Lord is to be shaped by that model and enabled by that death. He "emptied himself" in order to make the Body of Christ a servant community living in harmony with each other and with the Lord of the Church.

Wouldn't it be wonderful if someone would take this powerful hymn and set it to captivating music? Then the whole Church could sing itself into a living, breathing demonstration of her Savior!

The Character of the Body of Christ

As the individual members of the Church celebrate the enabling model of the Savior, the Church reproduces the model in daily living—inside and outside the Church. One author explains it this way: "Christian spiritual formation is a matter of becoming the Song that we sing, the Story we tell. . . . It is a matter of being loyal to a Person and conformed to the Story that helps us negotiate the unending variety of conflicting loyalties that confront us throughout a lifetime."[3]

As the Church rehearses in song and word the story of her Model, she deepens her loyalty to her Lord. A transformation results, inspired by the Model and enabled by His death on the Cross. "We ourselves are to become the living texts of Christianity."[4] We are to become the living reminders of God's grace in a broken world.

The church at Philippi had forgotten the power of their confession of Jesus as Lord. Paul invited them to return to the adoration that brings transformation. He invited them, by the power of the Spirit, to live in a harmony that shares the same solid focus of the Master—to have the "same mind."

"Let the same mind be in you that was in Christ Jesus" (v. 5) uses a verb in the imperative, one that points to what we should do. The construction in Greek is plural. It is a command from the apostle to become persons in community whose lives truly follow Christ as model. The whole phrase refers to an outlook and perspective that affect the mind, the will, and the emotions. That perspective will determine the flow of the total life of the person (and the community) who loves the Lord supremely. He or she will show a consistency and integrity among mind, emotions, heart, will, and actions. That "same mind," "same love," "full accord," "[absence of] selfish ambition or conceit," "humility," and looking "to the interests of others" (vv. 2-4) will have wonderful results in the life of the Church.

According to 1:27-28, that unity will enable her to withstand all opposition. Her opponents will not intimidate the Church. That unity will enable the church community to be the suffering servants who share the "privilege" of suffering for the Savior (1:29). That unity and harmony will enable the Church to "work out . . . salvation with fear and trembling" (2:12).

It was a wonderful revelation to me the day I recognized that "work out your own salvation" in verse 12 was in the plural in the original language. It is a call for the church *community* to so follow Christ that the church *community* is able to absorb its diversity in its common allegiance to Christ. What a powerful lesson!

They will accomplish all of this through the divine energizing. "This is God's doing" (1:28). "For it is God who is at work in you" (2:13). What a beautiful picture of the Church living out her call to follow Jesus through the enabling that God alone provides.

In Ephesians, Paul pictured this community unity and harmony in an intricate series of metaphors:

> Be *filled with the Spirit*, as you *sing* psalms and hymns and spiritual songs among yourselves, singing and making melody to the Lord in your hearts, *giving thanks* to God the Father at all times and for everything in the name of our Lord Jesus Christ. *Be subject* to one another out of *reverence* for Christ (5:18-21, *emphasis added*).

The enabling energy of God provided by the Spirit results in inner harmony individually and outer harmony in the church community. These are visible in the singing, in the thankfulness, and in the submission to each other "out of reverence for Christ." Surely these verses clarify the essence of the passage in Philippians.

In the last 13 years of teaching spiritual formation in a

seminary setting, I have become aware that the harmony of voices in singing increases in beauty as the group draws closer to Christ and to each other. We do indeed sing our way into conformity to our Lord—as individuals and as a church community.

Conclusion

This close look at Paul's Christological "hymn" has pointed to several questions that we can ask ourselves—both individually and corporately. The answers to these questions may reveal if our spiritual community has "the same mind . . . that was in Christ Jesus."

- How does adoration of the Savior shape your individual life?
- How does adoration of the Savior shape the life of your local congregation?
- How does common allegiance to Christ as the enabling Model shape the way your local Body of Christ handles diversity?
- How do you draw upon the enabling grace of God to become more Christlike?
- How does your local congregation draw upon the enabling grace of God to become more Christlike?
- What are the evidences of growing Christlikeness in your life?
- What are such evidences in the life of your local congregation?
- What are the songs most often sung in your congregation? How does that selection determine the shape of the community?

Searching for honest answers to the above questions will reveal where we fall short of living up to the Model Jesus provided. As we are willing to "empty" ourselves of all but what the Savior desires for us, the Spirit will enable us to celebrate Christ, as Paul did, with the "hymn" of our lives.

At the close of a chapel service in which the Word came alive in the minister's hand, I stood at attention as the organist played the postlude. Words and music written more than a century ago sprang to life in my heart. Tears began to flow as I meditated on the words:

One holy passion filling all my frame;

. . . .

My heart an altar, and Thy love the flame.[5]

When following Christ becomes our highest priority and passion—as individuals and as a community of believers—then God can use us to sing our world into a redemptive future.

About the author: Morris A. Weigelt, Ph.D., is professor of New Testament and spiritual formation at Nazarene Theological Seminary in Kansas City.

Notes

1. Gareth Weldon Icenogle, *Biblical Foundations for Small Group Ministry: An Integrational Approach* (Downer's Grove, Ill.: InterVarsity Press, 1994), 292.

2. Unless indicated otherwise, all Scripture quotations come from the New Revised Standard Version (NRSV).

3. Susanne Johnson, *Christian Spiritual Formation in the Church and Classroom* (Nashville: Abingdon, 1989), 117.

4. Ibid., 103.

5. George Croly, "Spirit of God, Descend upon My Heart," *Sing to the Lord* (Kansas City: Lillenas Publishing Co., 1993), 298.

Revelation 21—22

INTRODUCTION

Our tour of salvation history is winding down. The end is in sight. As we open the final pages of Revelation, another glorious vision meets us—the fulfillment of salvation history.

The apostle John wrote Revelation in his waning years on earth, probably around A.D. 95. The book is filled with visions that often seem bizarre to modern readers. To understand Revelation, readers must realize that it is a distinct type of literature. The material in Revelation is *apocalyptic* (from a Greek word meaning "reveal"), which is a highly symbolic type of writing.

What chapters 21 and 22 reveal, however, about a new heaven and new earth is really not so hard to understand. In fact, the descriptions inspire glorious thoughts of what the end of time will be like.

In a sense, Revelation 21—22 brings us "full circle" along our time line of salvation history. We started in the Garden of Eden, where perfection became tainted by sinning humans. We have traveled through the pages of the Old Testament where God revealed himself and set the plan of redemption in motion. We have journeyed through New Testament passages where we have witnessed the story of salvation in a flesh-and-blood Jesus. Now we get a glimpse of what complete Garden-of-Eden-perfect restoration will look like.

It seemed like the right choice for the Early Church fathers to place Revelation as the concluding book of the New Testament canon. Revelation 21—22 seems like the right place for us to conclude our overview of salvation as well.

CHAPTER 13

The New Beginning of Our Story

by Roger L. Hahn

A GOOD BOOK ALWAYS HAS A GOOD BEGINNING and a good ending. The author did not write the Book of Revelation just to be a good book, yet it qualifies on literary as well as on theological grounds. The final two chapters of Revelation bring the amazing visions of this book to a dramatic climax.

It is no accident that Revelation is the final book of the Christian Bible. The climactic vision that brings this book to a close also brings the whole story of salvation history to its glorious conclusion. The powerful promises of the all-sufficient grace of God in Christ found on these pages have spoken words of comfort and hope in every age of Christian history.

Revelation 21 and 22 contain the climax of the book. Some interpreters believe these chapters form a single literary unit. However, it is much more commonly thought (and more likely) that Revelation 21:1—22:5 presents the final vision that God revealed to John, the author of this book. The remainder of chapter 22 then presents a benediction relating to the Book of Revelation (and the Bible) as a whole and not just to the vision of 21:1—22:5.

The Final Vision

The content of John's final vision is found in Revelation 21:1—22:5. These verses actually report the vision twice. The first eight verses of chapter 21 provide a preview of the vision, and then Revelation 21:9—22:5 report the details of the vision. Though the two sections are separate, their contents overlap. Some details are most clearly expressed in the preview, but the majority find expression in the exposition that follows.

The Vision Previewed

The preview begins with the announcement that John saw "a new heaven and a new earth." The language comes from Isaiah 65:17, where God announces to the prophet that He is about to create a new heaven and a new earth. In the context of Isaiah, this spoke of a transformation of the present world into a place where sorrow and tragedy will be no more. In the time between the Old and New Testaments, various Jewish writers used the same terms to refer to the renewal of this earth and heaven to its original created holiness and glory. Other Jewish writers spoke of the complete destruction of the present earth and heaven. They saw the new creation as completely different from the present realities.

The first question confronting the reader of Revelation 21:1 is, Which (if either) of these Jewish ways of thinking influenced John's thought about the new heaven and the new earth? A modern interpreter is inclined to think that John saw a different heaven and earth since he spoke of the first ones as having passed away. Such a view may be true, but Isaiah 65:17 had also spoken of "former things" no longer being remembered. It is possible that John's vision pointed to a transformation of our present heaven and earth.

At first glance the description of there being no sea would favor the view that the new heaven and earth were different realities rather than merely the present existence transformed. However, the sea frequently was understood in symbolic as well as literal ways in Revelation particularly and the whole Bible generally. The beast of Revelation 13 had come out of the sea. Terrible beasts arose from the sea in Daniel 7. The nations around Old Testament Israel understood the sea as the place of chaos. The creation account of Genesis 1 shows God overcoming the chaos of the sea by putting it in its place. For a Jewish author the sea represented chaos and evil, and John was seeing a place where such a sea was no more.

Regardless of one's interpretation of the new heaven and new earth, John's only concern with them was a new city—the New Jerusalem. The rest of the vision focuses on this new and holy city. Verse 2 describes it "as a bride adorned for her husband." This is an important clue that John was thinking of a spiritual reality instead of (or in addition to) a literal city. The exposition beginning in verse 9 will give further insights from this spiritual perspective. A loud voice from the throne then interprets the significance of the vision in verses 3-4. These words echo with Old Testament allusions and meter, but with no direct quotations. The first comment about the New Jerusalem is, "Behold, the tabernacle of God is with men" (v. 3, NKJV). The word "tabernacle" echoes the language used in Exodus through 1 Samuel for Israel's portable worship center. The word literally means a tent. Its Greek root means a dwelling place, yet it sounds like a Hebrew word for "glory," *shekinah*. The second phrase builds on the first, "He [God] will dwell with them" (v. 3, NKJV). The word "dwell" is the same word that appears in John 1:14, "The Word became flesh and dwelt among us" (NKJV). The language then shifts to echoes of the Old Testament covenant formula, "I will be their God and they will be my people" (v. 3, author's translation).

Further, according to verse 4, "God will wipe away every tear" (NKJV). Death, grief, crying, and pain will be no more. These words from heaven clearly focus on a spiritual

and relational understanding of the New Jerusalem. T
most important part of that holy city is that God has com.
to be with His people and to live in covenant relationship
with them. Following the horrible persecution of the
Church that previous chapters of Revelation have described, the end of death and grief is a promise of a new reality almost beyond human imagination.

The paragraph found in verses 5-8 is unique in that it
is the only place in Revelation in which God himself is the
speaker. This fact gives special significance to the message
of these verses. Maybe we are to understand the vision to
be that of God introducing the Bride since these verses
connect both back to the preview of the Bride in verse 2
and forward to the exposition on the Bride in verses 9 and
following. The content of verses 5-8 is primarily pastoral—
assuring the truth of the vision, promising participation in
that coming new world to those who are faithful, and
warning of the doom that will befall those who persist in
the ways of the Antichrist. The language of verse 8, describing the many kinds of sinners, echoes descriptions of
the evil activities of the beast described in Revelation 13.
Faithful followers of Christ need not fear these evil doers
any longer, for their doom is sure.

The New Jerusalem as Bride of Christ

The exposition of the vision begins in Revelation 21:9.
In the process of further revealing the vision, allusions to
parts of Revelation other than 21:1-8 appear. Verse 9 provides an example. The agent revealing the vision becomes
one of the seven angels who had the seven bowls. The very
words describing the angel echo Revelation 17:1, and we
realize that part of the significance of the Holy City being
revealed in this final vision is its contrast to the harlot city,
Babylon, described in Revelation 17—18. The harlot city
sits on the beast from hell and exhibits all the unholy char-

...er of the devil. The Holy City comes down from heaven ...nd is the creation of God.

This city is the Bride, the wife of the Lamb. For the sake of any who may have missed the relational and spiritual purpose of this vision in the preview, it is now made clear in 21:9. The Bride is also described as the wife. This terminology is sometimes confusing to people of Western culture. We tend to use two words with reference to different periods of time in our relationships. We use *fiancé* during the engagement period and *husband* or *wife* after the marriage. However, in the biblical world the betrothal was such a binding arrangement that the words *husband* and *wife* could be used even before the wedding ceremony. The Old Testament had used the language of husband and wife to describe God and Israel in Isaiah 54:5 and Hosea 1—2. The parables of Jesus and the teaching of the apostles compare Christ and the Church to husband and wife. (See Matthew 22:1-14; 25:1-13; Mark 2:19-20; John 3:29; 2 Corinthians 11:2; and Ephesians 5:25-33.) The Bride of the Lamb is the Church, and she has already been introduced in Revelation 19:7-8, where the marriage of the Lamb is announced. Now in this final vision, the Bride descends the curved stairway from heaven to be joined to her eternal Husband at the forever marriage banquet of the Lamb.

Having made clear what the symbolism of the New Jerusalem refers to, the vision continues in the rest of the exposition. The city (the Church) possesses the glory of God and has a radiance like a rare jewel. A great wall with 12 gates surrounds it, with an angel at each gate. The names of the 12 tribes of Israel are written on the gates. Further, the wall has 12 foundations with each foundation bearing the name of one of the 12 apostles of the Lamb. An angel takes John on a measuring tour of the city. Its shape is a perfect cube 12,000 stadia in length, width, and height. That would be approximately 1,500 miles, but using mile

measurements misses the connection to the significa
number 12.

The dimensions of the city are beyond human comprehension. No city of human history has ever come close to occupying an area of 1,500 miles by 1,500 miles. Such a vast territory would encompass about half of the land area of the United States of America. Beyond that, the Holy City extends upward by the same dimension. Clearly, we must understand these numbers in terms of their symbolism.

The perfect cube calls to mind the holy of holies in the Temple and the tabernacle. Scripture describes nothing else as a cube. This is a way for the vision to make clear that the city is about the presence of God. Because of that holy presence, nothing unclean nor unholy may ever enter the cube—whether it is the holy of holies in the Temple or the coming city, the Bride of the Lamb.

The immense size suggests at least two truths. This city will have room for everyone—no overcrowding and no one left out for lack of space. Second, such dimensions would have included virtually all of the known world at that time. In a way that the Roman Empire could not accomplish, the boundaries between Jews and Gentiles, between barbarians and the civilized would disappear. Every nation, every people, and every language group would be welcome in this city (that is, the Church).

The wall of the city measured 144 cubits. Our equivalent would be approximately 216 feet, but again we need to retain the connection to that important number, 12, since the wall is 12 times 12 cubits. Most commentators conclude that the wall measurement refers to its thickness since the city's height is 12,000 stadia. Some, however, take the 144-cubit measurement to be the height of the wall, which yields two fascinating comparisons. First, in terms of an absolute number, a wall 216 feet high would have been impossibly high for the ancient world. It would speak of unassailable security for the city. On the other hand, compared the 1,500-mile height of the city, a 216-foot wall is almost nothing.

The vision, however, is more interested in the material of the wall than in its dimensions. It was built of jasper with 12 kinds of precious jewels adorning the foundation of the wall. The 12 gates are 12 pearls, and the city street is of pure gold. Any attempt to understand this description of the city literally goes beyond human ability to understand. A more understandable interpretation lies in how we are to take it as symbolism. A likely key to understanding the symbols comes from the repeated reference to the foundations of the wall in verses 14 and 19. In verse 14, the 12 foundations are inscribed with the names of the 12 apostles. In verses 19-20 the foundations are adorned with 12 precious jewels. The meaning of verse 14 is the easier to see. The Holy City (the Church) is built on the foundation of the testimony to Christ made by the 12 apostles. By the time John wrote Revelation, several heresies were beginning to threaten the Church. The final vision of the book declares that the Church rests on the testimony of the 12 apostles rather than the speculations of human philosophers.

The meaning of the 12 precious stones in the foundation is more difficult to discern. The simplest interpretation would be that each precious stone represents an apostle. However, some have attempted to connect these stones to the 12 precious stones on the high priest's breastplate (Exodus 28:17-21).

The Glorious Worship in That City

Moving from the exterior to the inside of the city, John commented in verse 22 that he saw no temple. In an ancient city such an omission would have been unthinkable, but no one needs a temple in this holy city. The temple of that city is the Lord God Almighty and the Lamb. At this point, the vision John saw is thoroughly consistent with the rest of the New Testament's understanding of the temple. In John 2:21 Jesus had described the true temple as own body. In his final sermon, Stephen had declared the God does not dwell in houses or temples made by human hands. In several passages the Epistle writers spoke of the Church as the temple of the Holy Spirit or God's own temple. (See 1 Corinthians 3:16; Ephesians 2:21; and 1 Peter 2:5.) Had the vision taken the direction of Paul and Peter, the Holy City itself as the Church would have been the temple. However, the vision follows the line of Jesus' teaching that He would become the temple himself. All that the old Temple included and anticipated for meeting God is fulfilled in the New Jerusalem, where God and His people dwell together forever.

The glorious description of the Holy City continues in verses 23-27. There is no need of sun or moon, for the glory of God is the light of that city. The symbolism here is similar to that used by Jesus in John 8:12 when He declared, "I *am* the light of the world" (emphasis added). The Old Testament images of the brightness of Shekinah glory also come into play here. There may also be echoes of the creation story of Genesis 1:3-5 and 14-19 where God spoke light and the sun, moon, and stars into existence. In the first earth, light existed by the power of God's *word*. In the new heaven and earth, light exists by the glory of God's *presence*. Verse 24 draws on the prophecy of Isaiah 60:1-7 but modifies it by making the glory of God and of the Lamb the goal of the nations and rulers who flow toward the city. Verse 25 declares that its gates will never be shut in the day, and there is no night there. That the gates would always be open wide speaks of two important truths about the city. One is that security is not a problem because there is no more fear in that city. What a glorious promise for the Church—a day when we live without fear! Second, the wide-open gates show that the city (the Church) is open to all; none are excluded by reason of their race, culture, or nationality.

However, nothing and no one sinful will enter the city, according to verse 27. The vision does not say what it is that keeps evil out of the city, but it is not fear, nor the gates, nor the wall. From the context we might infer that the blinding glory of God's presence is more than sin can bear to look at, let alone be around forever. This section offers a glorious word of promise to the Church about a day that is coming when we will no longer need to fear the infiltration of sin into our midst or into our own lives. Of course, this vision also should cause us to examine our own hearts as to whether our devotion to Christ is so complete that we can comfortably dwell in His glorious holiness eternally.

The final paragraph in the final vision—Revelation 22:1-5—is also set inside the Holy City. The angel shows John the river of the water of life flowing from the throne of God and of the Lamb. This river flows down the center of the street of the city. These verses echo elements of the description of the river of Ezekiel 47 that flows from beneath the threshold of the Temple. Healing and life-giving qualities are common to both rivers. Many scholars also hear an echo of the river flowing through the Garden of Eden as described in Genesis 2:9-10. The reference to the tree of life in Revelation 22:2 heightens the return to the Genesis scene. This is a glorious picture of the Holy City completing in the new heaven and new earth the final stage in the plan of salvation history. These verses bring us full circle back to God's original intention for human beings when He created us. John's vision is of God's people someday being a community in which nothing accursed can be found. It will be a community that serves and worships God as He created us to do (v. 3). It will be a community that will reign with Christ forever (v. 5). This promise is beautifully expressed in verse 4 with the statement that God's people will see God's face. The intimacy of the Garden of Eden in which the original couple walked and talked with the Lord in the cool of the evening will be restored in face-to-face communion with God. The banishment of Cain from both the garden and God's presence will be reversed, and God's name will be written on His people's foreheads. The biblical connection of name and nature suggests that God's own nature will come to mark the lives of His people.

The Benediction

Benediction is the term for the sentence in verse 7, "Blessed is he who keeps the words of the prophecy of this book" (NKJV). Verse 14 is a benediction as well. However, benediction is also an appropriate description for the final 16 verses of Revelation. The book has offered a continual invitation to worship throughout its pages. The final words following the concluding vision are much more than just a haphazard collection of religious thoughts, as some have claimed. These closing verses pronounce the benediction on the worship experience of reading Revelation. They also invite us to both further and future worship around the throne and the Lamb.

Verses 6, 18, and 19 affirm the validity of the visions of the book. The words of Revelation are reliable and trustworthy. Their truth is guaranteed because they speak a message from the trustworthy and reliable God whom we worship. There is no invitation to worship the book or the visions. The concluding benediction of Revelation issues the call in verse 9 to worship God.

This worship concludes with a twofold invitation. First, this benediction invites the reader to a life of holiness and faithfulness. The blessing of verse 7 is on the person who "keeps the words of the prophecy of this book" (NKJV). The blessing of verse 14 is on those who wash their robes to gain access to the tree of life. These words are a clear call to a holy life that begins now and grows in its openness to God's presence until the barriers of this earth

that separate us from God will finally disappear. Verses 10-11 exhort us that the time is short. We have no need to seal up the book and put it in storage. Those who are set in wicked ways will remain in their wicked ways, and those who are committed to righteousness and holiness are called to remain righteous and holy for the short interval that remains.

Even more prominent and poignant than the invitation to holiness to us, the readers, is the invitation extended to Christ to return for His waiting Church. In verse 17 both the Bride that is the Church and the Spirit call out, "Come." In verse 20 the author invites, "Come, Lord Jesus!" Beyond doubt, this prayer for Christ's return was on the lips of the first readers of Revelation. The threat of persecution and death in their times gave special power to the prayer. However, from the earliest days, Christ's Church has expressed its longing for His presence in the words, "Come, Lord Jesus!" No other words could be more appropriate as the final words of both Revelation and the Bible as a whole.

One other theme in this closing benediction is even stronger than the Church's fervent prayer for Christ's return. That is our Lord's promise that, in fact, He is coming. Verses 7, 12, and 20 announce in a glad refrain, "I am coming soon." These final words of Scripture are the whispers of the waiting Bride, "Come, Lord Jesus!" and the Bridegroom, "Yes! I am coming soon." With eager and bated breath we now live anticipating the Marriage Supper of the Lamb!

About the author: Roger L. Hahn, Ph.D., is professor of New Testament at Nazarene Theological Seminary in Kansas City.